shakespeare's
macbeth

shakespeare's
macbeth

harold bloom

riverhead books
new york

THE BERKLEY PUBLISHING GROUP
Published by the Penguin Group
Penguin Group (USA) Inc.
375 Hudson Street, New York, New York 10014, U.S.A.
Penguin Group (Canada), 10 Alcorn Avenue, Toronto, Ontario, Canada M4V 3B2
(a division of Pearson Penguin Canada Inc.)
Penguin Books Ltd., 80 Strand, London WC2R 0RL, England
Penguin Group Ireland, 25 St. Stephen's Green, Dublin 2, Ireland (a division of Penguin
Books, Ltd.)
Penguin Group (Australia), 250 Camberwell Road, Camberwell, Victoria 3124, Australia
(a division of Pearson Australia Group Pty., Ltd.)
Penguin Books India Pvt. Ltd., 11 Community Centre, Panchsheel Park, New Delhi-
110 017, India
Penguin Group (NZ), Cnr. Airborne and Rosedale Roads, Albany, Auckland, New Zealand
(a division of Pearson New Zealand, Ltd.)
Penguin Books (South Africa) (Pty.) Ltd., 24 Sturdee Avenue, Rosebank, Johannesburg
2196, South Africa

Penguin Books Ltd., Registered Offices: 80 Strand, London, WC2R 0RL, England

PRINTING HISTORY
Riverhead trade paperback edition: October 2004

Library of Congress Cataloging-in-Publication Data

Bloom, Harold.
  Shakespeare's Macbeth / Harold Bloom—1st Riverhead trade pbk. ed.
    p. cm.
The essay "Macbeth" was previously published as part of Shakespeare : invention of
the human, by Harold Bloom, published by Riverhead in 1998.
  Includes the full text of the play, with editorial revisions by Harold Bloom.
  ISBN 1-59448-008-7
    1. Shakespeare, William, 1564–1616. Macbeth. 2. Macbeth, King of Scotland, 11th
cent.—In literature. 3. Macbeth, King of Scotland, 11th cent.—Drama. 4. Scotland—
Kings and rulers—Drama. 5. Kings and rulers in literature. 6. Scotland—In literature.
7. Regicides in literature. 8. Regicides—Drama.   I. Shakespeare, William, 1564–1616.
Macbeth. II. Bloom, Harold. Shakespeare. III. Title.

PR2823.B56 2004
822.3'3—dc22   2004050848

PRINTED IN THE UNITED STATES OF AMERICA

10 9 8 7 6 5 4 3 2 1

contents

The text of *Macbeth,* including the synopsis, is that of the old Cambridge Edition (1893), as edited by William Aldis Wright. I am grateful to Brett Foster for indispensable advice upon the editorial revisions I have made in the text.

—Harold Bloom

harold bloom on
macbeth

Theatrical tradition has made *Macbeth* the unluckiest of all Shakespeare's plays, particularly for those who act in it. Macbeth himself can be termed the unluckiest of all Shakespearean protagonists, precisely because he is the most imaginative. A great killing machine, Macbeth is endowed by Shakespeare with something less than ordinary intelligence, but with a power of fantasy so enormous that pragmatically it seems to be Shakespeare's own. No other drama by Shakespeare—not even *King Lear, A Midsummer Night's Dream,* or *The Tempest*—so engulfs us in a phantasmagoria. The magic in *A Midsummer Night's Dream* and *The Tempest* is crucially effectual, while there is no overt magic or witchcraft in *King Lear,* though we sometimes half expect it because the drama is of such hallucinatory intensity.

The witchcraft in *Macbeth,* though pervasive, cannot alter material events, yet hallucination can and does. The rough magic in *Macbeth* is wholly Shakespeare's; he indulges his own imagination as never before, seeking to find its moral limits (if any). I do not suggest that Macbeth represents Shakespeare, in any of the complex ways that Falstaff and Hamlet may represent certain inner aspects of the playwright. But in the Renaissance sense of imagination (which is not ours), Macbeth may well be the emblem of that faculty in Shakespeare, a faculty that must have frightened Shakespeare and ought to terrify us, when we read or attend *Macbeth,* for the play depends upon its horror of its own imaginings. Imagination (or fancy) is an equivocal matter for Shakespeare and his era, where it meant both poetic furor, as a kind of substitute for divine inspiration, and a gap torn in reality, almost a punishment for the displacement of the sacred into the secular. Shakespeare somewhat mitigates the negative aura of fantasy in his other plays, but not in *Macbeth,* which is a tragedy of the imagination. Though the play triumphantly proclaims, "The time is free," when Macbeth is killed, the reverberations we cannot escape as we leave the theater or close the book have little to do with our freedom.

Hamlet dies into freedom, perhaps even augmenting our own liberty, but Macbeth's dying is less of a release for us. The universal reaction to Macbeth is that we identify with him, or at least with his imagination. Richard III, Iago, and Edmund are hero-villains; to call Macbeth one of that company seems all wrong. They delight in their wickedness; Macbeth suffers intensely from knowing that he does evil, and that he must go on doing ever worse. Shakespeare rather dreadfully sees to it that *we are* Macbeth; our identity with him is involuntary but inescapable. All of us possess, to one degree or another, a proleptic imagination; in Macbeth, it is absolute. He scarcely is conscious of an ambition, desire, or wish before he *sees* himself on the other side or shore, already having performed the crime that equivocally fulfills ambition. Macbeth terrifies us partly because that aspect of our own imagination is so frightening: it seems to make us murderers, thieves, usurpers, and rapists.

Why are we unable to resist identifying with Macbeth? He so

dominates his play that we have nowhere else to turn. Lady Macbeth is a powerful character, but Shakespeare gets her off the stage after Act III, Scene iv, except for her short return in a state of madness at the start of Act V. Shakespeare had killed off Mercutio early to keep him from stealing *Romeo and Juliet,* and had allowed Falstaff only a reported death scene so as to prevent Sir John from dwarfing the "reformed" Hal in *Henry V.* Once Lady Macbeth has been removed, the only real presence on the stage is Macbeth's. Shrewdly, Shakespeare does little to individualize Duncan, Banquo, Macduff, and Malcolm. The drunken porter, Macduff's little son, and Lady Macduff are more vivid in their brief appearances than are all the secondary males in the play, who are wrapped in a common grayness. Since Macbeth speaks fully a third of the drama's lines, and Lady Macbeth's role is truncated, Shakespeare's design upon us is manifest. We are to journey inward to Macbeth's heart of darkness, and there we will find ourselves more truly and more strange, murderers in and of the spirit.

The terror of this play, most ably discussed by Wilbur Sanders, is deliberate and salutary. If we are compelled to identify with Macbeth, and he appalls us (and himself), then we ourselves must be fearsome also. Working against the Aristotelian formula for tragedy, Shakespeare deluges us with fear and pity, not to purge us but for a sort of purposiveness without purpose that no interpretation wholly comprehends. The sublimity of Macbeth and of Lady Macbeth is overwhelming: they are persuasive and valuable personalities, profoundly in love with each other. Indeed, with surpassing irony Shakespeare presents them as the happiest married couple in all his work. And they are anything but two fiends, despite their dreadful crimes and deserved catastrophes. So rapid and foreshortened is their play (about half the length of *Hamlet*) that we are given no leisure to confront their descent into hell as it happens. Something vital in us is bewildered by the evanescence of their better natures, though Shakespeare gives us emblems enough of the way down and out.

Macbeth is an uncanny unity of setting, plot, and characters, fused together beyond comparison with any other play of Shakespeare's. The drama's cosmos is more drastic and alienated even than *King Lear's,* where nature was so radically wounded. *King Lear* was pre-Christian, whereas *Macbeth,* overtly medieval Catholic, seems less set in Scotland than in the *kenoma,* the cosmological emptiness of our world as described by the ancient Gnostic heretics. Shakespeare knew at least something of gnosticism through the Hermetic philosophy of Giordano Bruno, though I think there can be little or no possibility of a direct influence of Bruno on Shakespeare (despite the interesting surmises of Frances Yates). Yet the gnostic horror of time seems to have infiltrated *Macbeth,* emanating from the not-less-than-universal nature of Shakespeare's own consciousness. The world of *Macbeth* is one into which we *have been thrown,* a dungeon for tyrants and victims alike. If *Lear* was pre-Christian, then *Macbeth* is weirdly post-Christian. There are, as we have seen, Christian intimations that haunt the pagans of *Lear,* though to no purpose or effect. Despite some desperate allusions by several of the characters, *Macbeth* allows no relevance to Christian revelation. Macbeth is the deceitful "man of blood" abhorred by the Psalms and elsewhere in the Bible, but he scarcely can be assimilated to biblical villainy. There is nothing specifically anti-Christian in his crimes; they would offend virtually every vision of the sacred and the moral that human chronicle has known. That may be why Akira Kurosawa's *Throne of Blood* is so uncannily the most successful film version of *Macbeth,* though it departs very far from the specifics of Shakespeare's play. Macbeth's tragedy, like Hamlet's, Lear's, and Othello's, is so universal that a strictly Christian context is inadequate to it.

I have ventured several times in this book my surmise that

Shakespeare intentionally evades (or even blurs) Christian categories throughout his work. He is anything but a devotional poet and dramatist; there are no *Holy Sonnets* by Shakespeare. Even Sonnet 146 ("Poor soul, the centre of my sinful earth") is an equivocal poem, particularly in its crucial eleventh line: "Buy terms divine in selling hours of dross." One major edition of Shakespeare glosses "terms divine" as "everlasting life," but "terms" allows several less ambitious readings. Did Shakespeare "believe in" the resurrection of the body? We cannot know, but I find nothing in the plays or poems to suggest a consistent supernaturalism in their author, and more perhaps to intimate a pragmatic nihilism. There is no more spiritual comfort to be gained from *Macbeth* than from the other high tragedies. Graham Bradshaw subtly argues that the *terrors* of *Macbeth* are Christian, yet he also endorses Nietzsche's reflections on the play in Nietzsche's *Daybreak* (1881). Here is section 240 of *Daybreak*:

On the morality of the stage.—Whoever thinks that Shakespeare's theatre has a moral effect, and that the sight of Macbeth irresistibly repels one from the evil of ambition, is in error: and he is again in error if he thinks Shakespeare himself felt as he feels. He who is really possessed by raging ambition beholds this its image with *joy,* and if the hero perishes by his passion this precisely is the sharpest spice in the hot draught of this joy. Can the poet have felt otherwise? How royally, and not at all like a rogue, does his ambitious man pursue his course from the moment of his great crime! Only from then on does he exercise 'demonic' attraction and excite similar natures to emulation—demonic means here: in defiance *against* life and advantage for the sake of a drive and idea. Do you suppose that Tristan and Isolde are preaching *against* adultery when they both perish by it? This would be to stand the poets on their head: they, and especially Shakespeare, are enamoured of the passions as such and not least of their death-welcoming moods—those moods in which the heart adheres to life no more firmly than does a drop of water to a glass. It is not the guilt and its evil outcome they have at heart, Shakespeare as little as Sophocles (in Ajax, Philoctetes, Oedipus): as easy as it would have been in these instances to make guilt the lever of the drama, just as surely has this been avoided. The tragic poet has just as little desire to take sides *against* life with his images of life! He cries rather: 'it is the stimulant of stimulants, this exciting, changing, dangerous, gloomy and often sun-drenched existence! It is an adventure to live—espouse what party in it you will, it will always retain this character!'—He speaks thus out of a restless, vigorous age which is half-drunk and stupefied by its excess of blood and energy—out of a wickeder age than ours is: which is why we need first to *adjust* and *justify* the goal of a Shakespearean drama, that is to say, not to understand it.

Nietzsche links up here with William Blake's adage that the highest art is immoral, and that "Exuberance is beauty." *Macbeth* certainly has "an excess of blood and energy"; its terrors may be more Christian than Greek or Roman, but indeed they are so primordial that they seem to me more shamanistic than Christian, even as the "terms divine" of Sonnet 146 impress me as rather more Platonic than Christian. Of all Shakespeare's plays, *Macbeth* is most "a tragedy of blood," not just in its murders but in the ultimate implications of Macbeth's imagination itself being bloody. The usurper Macbeth moves in a consistent phantasmagoria of blood: blood is the prime constituent of his imagination. He *sees* that what opposes him is blood in one aspect—call it nature in the sense that he opposes nature—and that this opposing force thrusts him into shedding more blood: "It will have blood, they say: blood will have blood."

Macbeth speaks these words in the aftermath of confronting Banquo's ghost, and as always his imaginative coherence overcomes his cognitive confusion. "It" is blood as the natural—call that King Duncan—and the second "blood" is all that Macbeth can experience. His usurpation of Duncan transcends the politics of the kingdom, and threatens a natural good deeply embedded in the Macbeths, but which they have abandoned, and which Macbeth now seeks to destroy, even upon the cosmological level, if only he could. You can call this natural good or first sense of "blood" Christian, if you want to, but Christianity is a revealed religion, and Macbeth rebels against nature *as he imagines it.* That pretty much makes Christianity as irrelevant to *Macbeth* as it is to *King Lear,* and indeed to all the Shakespearean tragedies. Othello, a Christian convert, does not fall away from Christianity but from his own better nature, while Hamlet is the apotheosis of all natural gifts, yet cannot abide in them. I am not suggesting, here as elsewhere in the book, that Shakespeare himself was a gnostic, or a nihilist, or a Nietzschean vitalist three centuries before Nietzsche. But as a dramatist, he is just as much all or any of those as he is a Christian. *Macbeth,* as I have intimated before, is anything but a celebration of Shakespeare's imagination, yet it is also anything but a Christian tragedy. Shakespeare, who understood everything that we comprehend and far more (humankind never will stop catching up to him), long since had exorcised Marlowe, and Christian tragedy (however inverted) with him. Macbeth has nothing in common with Tamburlaine or with Faustus. The nature that Macbeth most strenuously violates is his own, but though he learns this even as he begins the violation, he refuses to follow Lady Macbeth into madness and suicide.

2

Like *A Midsummer Night's Dream* and *The Tempest, Macbeth* is a visionary drama, and difficult as it is for us to accept that strange genre, a visionary tragedy. Macbeth himself is an involuntary seer, almost an occult medium, dreadfully open to the spirits of the air and of the night. Lady Macbeth, initially more enterprising than her husband, falls into a psychic decline for causes more visionary than not. So much are the Macbeths made for sublimity, figures of fiery eros as they are, that their political and dynastic ambitions seem grotesquely inadequate to their mutual desires. Why do they want the crown? Shakespeare's Richard III, still Marlovian, seeks the sweet fruition of an earthly crown, but the Macbeths are not Machiavellian overreachers, nor are they sadists or power-obsessed as such. Their mutual lust is also a lust for the throne, a desire that is their Nietzschean revenge against time and time's irrefutable declaration: "It was." Shakespeare did not care to clarify the Macbeths' childlessness. Lady Macbeth speaks of having nursed a child, presumably her own but now dead; we are not told that Macbeth is her second husband, but we may take him to be that. He urges her to bring forth men children only, in admiration of her "manly" resolve, yet pragmatically they seem to expect no heirs of their own union, while he fiercely seeks to murder Fleance, Banquo's son, and does destroy Macduff's children. Freud, shrewder on *Macbeth* than on *Hamlet,* called the curse of childlessness Macbeth's motivation for murder and usurpation. Shakespeare left this matter more uncertain; it is a little difficult to imagine Macbeth as a father when he is, at first, so profoundly dependent on Lady Macbeth. Until she goes mad, she seems as much Macbeth's mother as his wife.

Of all Shakespeare's tragic protagonists, Macbeth is the least free. As Wilbur Sanders implied, Macbeth's actions are a kind of falling forward ("falling in space," Sanders called it). Whether or not Nietzsche (and Freud after him) were right in believing that we are lived, thought, and willed by forces not ourselves, Shakespeare anticipated Nietzsche in this conviction. Sanders acutely follows Nietzsche in giving us a Macbeth who pragmatically lacks any will, in contrast to Lady Macbeth, who is a pure will until she breaks apart. Nietzsche's insight may be the clue to the different ways in which the Macbeths desire the crown: she wills it, he wills nothing, and paradoxically she collapses while he grows ever more frightening, outraging others, himself outraged, as he becomes the nothing he projects. And yet this nothingness remains a negative sublime; its grandeur merits the dignity of tragic perspectives. The enigma of *Macbeth,* as a drama, always will remain its protagonist's hold upon our terrified sympathy. Shakespeare surmised the guilty imaginings we share with Macbeth, who is Mr. Hyde to our Dr. Jekyll. Stevenson's marvelous story emphasizes that Hyde is younger than Jekyll, only because Jekyll's career is still young in villainy while old in good works. Our uncanny sense that Macbeth somehow is younger in deed than we are is analogous. Virtuous as we may (or may not) be, we fear that Macbeth, our Mr. Hyde, has the power to realize our own potential for active evil. Poor Jekyll eventually turns into Mr. Hyde and cannot get back; Shakespeare's art is to suggest we could have such a fate.

Is Shakespeare himself—on any level—also a Dr. Jekyll in relation to Macbeth's Mr. Hyde? How could he not be, given his success in touching a universal negative sublime through having imagined Macbeth's imaginings? Like Hamlet, with whom he has some curious affinities, Macbeth projects an aura of intimacy: with the audience, with the hapless actors, with his creator. Formalist critics of Shakespeare—old guard and new—insist that no character is larger than the play, since a character is "only" an actor's role. Audiences and readers are not so formalistic: Shylock,

Falstaff, Rosalind, Hamlet, Malvolio, Macbeth, Cleopatra (and some others) seem readily transferable to contexts different from their dramas. Sancho Panza, as Kafka demonstrated in the wonderful parable "The Truth About Sancho Panza," can become the creator of Don Quixote. Some new and even more Borgesian Kafka must rise among us to show Antonio as the inventor of Shylock, or Prince Hal as the father of Sir John Falstaff.

To call Macbeth larger than his play in no way deprecates my own favorite among all of Shakespeare's works. The economy of *Macbeth* is ruthless, and scholars who find it truncated, or partly the work of Thomas Middleton, fail to understand Shakespeare's darkest design. What notoriously dominates this play, more than any other in Shakespeare, is time, time that is not the Christian mercy of eternity, but devouring time, death nihilistically regarded as finality. No critic has been able to distinguish between death, time, and nature in *Macbeth;* Shakespeare so fuses them that all of us are well within the mix. We hear voices crying out the formulae of redemption, but never persuasively, compared with Macbeth's soundings of night and the grave. Technically, the men in *Macbeth* are "Christian warriors," as some critics like to emphasize, but their Scottish medieval Catholicism is perfunctory. The kingdom, as in *King Lear,* is a kind of cosmological waste land, a Creation that was also a Fall, in the beginning.

Macbeth is very much a night piece; its Scotland is more a mythological Northland than the actual nation from which Shakespeare's royal patron emerged. King James I doubtless prompted some of the play's emphases, but hardly the most decisive, the sense that the night has usurped the day. Murder is the characteristic action of *Macbeth:* not just King Duncan, Banquo, and Lady Macduff and her children are the victims. By firm implication, every person in the play is a potential target for the Macbeths. Shakespeare, who perhaps mocked the stage horrors of other dramatists in his *Titus Andronicus,* experimented far more subtly with the aura of murderousness in *Macbeth*. It is not so much that each of us in the audience is a potential victim. Rather more uneasily, the little Macbeth within each theatergoer can be tempted to surmise a murder or two of her or his own.

I can think of no other literary work with *Macbeth's* power of *contamination,* unless it be Herman Melville's *Moby-Dick,* the prose epic profoundly influenced by *Macbeth*. Ahab is another visionary maniac, obsessed with what seems a malign order in the universe. Ahab strikes through the mask of natural appearances, as Macbeth does, but the White Whale is no easy victim. Like Macbeth, Ahab is outraged by the equivocation of the fiend that lies like truth, and yet Ahab's prophet, the Parsi harpooner Fedallah, himself is far more equivocal than the Weird Sisters. We identify with Captain Ahab less ambivalently than we do with King Macbeth, since Ahab is neither a murderer nor a usurper, and yet pragmatically Ahab is about as destructive as Macbeth: all on the *Pequod,* except for Ishmael the narrator, are destroyed by Ahab's quest. Melville, a shrewd interpreter of Shakespeare, borrows Macbeth's phantasmagoric and proleptic imagination for Ahab, so that both Ahab and Macbeth become world destroyers. The Scottish heath and the Atlantic Ocean amalgamate: each is a context where preternatural forces have outraged a sublime consciousness, who fights back vainly and unluckily, and goes down to a great defeat. Ahab, an American Promethean, is perhaps more hero than villain, unlike Macbeth, who forfeits our admiration though not our entrapped sympathy.

3

Hazlitt remarked of Macbeth that "he is sure of nothing but the present moment." As the play progresses to its catastrophe, Macbeth loses even that certitude, and his apocalyptic anxieties prompt Victor Hugo's identification of Macbeth with Nimrod, the Bible's first hunter of men. Macbeth is worthy of the identification: his shocking vitality imbues the violence of evil with biblical force and majesty, giving us the paradox that the play seems Christian not for any benevolent expression but only insofar as its ideas of evil surpass merely naturalistic explanations. If any theology is applicable to *Macbeth,* then it must be the most negative of theologies, one that excludes the Incarnation. The cosmos of *Macbeth,* like that of *Moby-Dick,* knows no Savior; the heath and the sea alike are great shrouds, whose dead will not be resurrected.

God is exiled from *Macbeth* and *Moby-Dick,* and from *King Lear* also. Exiled, not denied or slain; Macbeth rules in a cosmological emptiness where God is lost, either too far away or too far within to be summoned back. As in *King Lear,* so in *Macbeth*: the moment of creation and the moment of fall fuse into one. Nature and man alike fall into time, even as they are created.

No one desires *Macbeth* to lose its witches, because of their dramatic immediacy, yet the play's cosmological vision renders them a little redundant.

Between what Macbeth imagines and what he does, there is only a temporal gap, in which he himself seems devoid of will. The Weird Sisters, Macbeth's Muses, take the place of that will; we cannot imagine them appearing to Iago, or to Edmund, both geniuses of the will. They are not hollow men; Macbeth is. What happens to Macbeth is inevitable, despite his own culpability, and no other play by Shakespeare, not even the early farces, moves with such speed (as Coleridge noted). Perhaps the rapidity augments the play's terror; there seems to be no power of the mind over the universe of death, a cosmos all but identical both with Macbeth's phantasmagoria and with the Weird Sisters.

Shakespeare grants little cognitive power to anyone in *Macbeth,* and least of all to the protagonist himself. The intellectual powers of Hamlet, Iago, and Edmund are not relevant to Macbeth and to his play. Shakespeare disperses the energies of the mind, so that no single character in *Macbeth* represents any particular capacity for understanding the tragedy, nor could they do better in concert. Mind is elsewhere in *Macbeth,* it has forsaken humans and witches alike, and lodges freestyle where it will, shifting capriciously and quickly from one corner of the sensible emptiness to another. Coleridge hated the Porter's scene (II.iii), with its famous knocking at the gate, but Coleridge made himself deaf to the cognitive urgency of the knocking. Mind knocks, and breaks into the play, with the first and only comedy allowed in this drama. Shakespeare employs his company's leading clown (presumably Robert Armin) to introduce a healing touch of nature where *Macbeth* has intimidated us with the preternatural, and with the Macbeths' mutual phantasmagoria of murder and power:

> *Porter.* Here's a knocking, indeed! If a man were Porter of Hell Gate, he should have old turning the key. *(Knocking.)* Knock, knock, knock. Who's there, i' th' name of Belzebub?—Here's a farmer, that hang'd himself on th' expectation of plenty: Come in time-server; have napkins enow about you; here you'll sweat for't.*(Knocking.)* Knock, knock. Who's there, i' th' other devil's name?—Faith, here's an equivocator, that could swear in both the scales against either scale; who committed treason enough for God's sake, yet could not equivocate to heaven: O! come in, equivocator. *(Knocking.)* Knock, knock, knock. Who's there?—Faith, here's an English tailor come hither for stealing out of a French hose: come in, tailor; here you may roast your goose. *(Knocking.)* Knock, knock. Never at quiet! What are you?—But this place is too cold for Hell. I'll devil-porter it no

further: I had thought to have let in some of all professions, that go the primrose way to th' everlasting bonfire.
(Knocking.) Anon, anon: I pray you, remember the Porter.

[II. iii. 1–22]

Cheerfully hungover, the Porter admits Macduff and Lennox
through what indeed is now Hell Gate, the slaughterhouse where
Macbeth has murdered the good Duncan. Shakespeare may well
be grimacing at himself on "a farmer, that hang'd himself on
th' expectation of plenty," since investing in grain was one of
Shakespeare's favorite risks of venture capital. The more profound humor comes in the proleptic contrast between the Porter
and Macbeth. As keeper of Hell Gate, the Porter boisterously
greets "an equivocator," presumably a Jesuit like Father Garnet,
who asserted a right to equivocal answers so as to avoid self-
incrimination in the Gunpowder Plot trial of early 1606, the year
Macbeth was first performed. Historicizing *Macbeth* as a reaction to
the Gunpowder Plot to me seems only a compounding of darkness with darkness, since Shakespeare always transcends commen-
tary on his own moment in time. We rather are meant to contrast
the hard-drinking Porter with Macbeth himself, who will remind
us of the Porter, but not until Act V, Scene v, when Birnam Wood
comes to Dunsinane and Macbeth begins: "To doubt th' equivocation of the fiend,/That lies like truth." De Quincey confined his
analysis of the knocking at the gate in Macbeth to the shock of the
four knocks themselves, but as an acute rhetorician he should have
attended more to the Porter's subsequent dialogue with Macduff,
where the Porter sends up forever the notion of "equivocation" by
expounding how alcohol provokes three things:

Porter. Marry, Sir, nose-painting, sleep, and urine. Lechery,
Sir, it provokes, and unprovokes: it provokes the desire,
but it takes away the performance. Therefore, much

drink may be said to be an equivocator with lechery: it
makes him, and it mars him; it sets him on, and it takes
him off; it persuades him, and disheartens him; makes
him stand to, and not stand to: in conclusion, equivocates him in a sleep, and giving him the lie, leaves him.

[II.iii.28–37]

Drunkenness is another equivocation, provoking lust but then
denying the male his capacity for performance. Are we perhaps
made to wonder whether Macbeth, like Iago, plots murderously
because his sexual capacity has been impaired? If you have a proleptic imagination as intense as Macbeth's, then your desire or
ambition outruns your will, reaching the other bank, or shoal, of
time all too quickly. The fierce sexual passion of the Macbeths
possesses a quality of baffled intensity, possibly related to their
childlessness, so that the Porter may hint at a situation that transcends his possible knowledge, but not the audience's surmises.

Macbeth's ferocity as a killing machine exceeds even the capacity of such great Shakespearean butchers as Aaron the Moor
and Richard III, or the heroic Roman battle prowess of Antony
and of Coriolanus. Iago's possible impotence would have some
relation to the humiliation of being passed over for Cassio. But
if Macbeth's manhood has been thwarted, there is no Othello
for him to blame; the sexual victimization, if it exists, is self-
generated by an imagination so impatient with time's workings
that it always overprepares every event. This may be an element
in Lady Macbeth's taunts, almost as if the manliness of Macbeth
can be restored only by his murder of the sleeping Duncan, whom
Lady Macbeth cannot slay because the good king resembles *her*
father in his slumber. The mounting nihilism of Macbeth, which
will culminate in his image of life as a tale signifying nothing,
perhaps then has more affinity with Iago's devaluation of reality
than with Edmund's cold potency.

A. C. Bradley found in *Macbeth* more of a "Sophoclean irony" than anywhere else in Shakespeare, meaning by such irony an augmenting awareness in the audience far exceeding the protagonist's consciousness that perpetually he is saying one thing, and meaning more than he himself understands in what he says. I agree with Bradley that *Macbeth* is the masterpiece of Shakespearean irony, which transcends dramatic, or Sophoclean, irony. Macbeth consistently says more than he knows, but he also imagines more than he says, so that the gap between his overt consciousness and his imaginative powers, wide to begin with, becomes extraordinary. Sexual desire, particularly in males, is likely to manifest all the vicissitudes of the drive when that abyss is so vast. This may be part of the burden of Lady Macbeth's lament before the banquet scene dominated by Banquo's ghost:

> Nought's had, all's spent,
> Where our desire is got without content:
> 'Tis safer to be that which we destroy,
> Than by destruction dwell in doubtful joy.
>
> [III.ii.4–7]

The madness of Lady Macbeth exceeds a trauma merely of guilt; her husband consistently turns from her (though never against her) once Duncan is slain. Whatever the two had intended by the mutual "greatness" they had promised each other, the subtle irony of Shakespeare reduces such greatness to a pragmatic desexualization once the usurpation of the crown has been realized. There is a fearful pathos in Lady Macbeth's cries of "To bed," in her madness, and a terrifying proleptic irony in her earlier outcry "Unsex me here." It is an understatement to aver that no other author's sense of human sexuality equals Shakespeare's in scope and in precision. The terror that we experience, as audience or as readers, when we suffer *Macbeth* seems to me, in many ways, sexual in its nature, if only because murder increasingly becomes Macbeth's mode of sexual expression. Unable to beget children, Macbeth slaughters them.

4

Though it is traditional to regard *Macbeth* as being uniquely terrifying among Shakespeare's plays, it will appear eccentric that I should regard this tragedy's fearsomeness as somehow sexual in its origins and in its dominant aspects. The violence of *Macbeth* doubtless impresses us more than it did the drama's contemporary audiences. Many if not most of those who attended *Macbeth* also joined the large crowds who thronged public executions in London, including drawings-and-quarterings as well as more civilized beheadings. The young Shakespeare, as we saw, probably heaped up outrages in his *Titus Andronicus* both to gratify his audience and to mock such gratification. But the barbarities of *Titus Andronicus* are very different in their effect from the savageries of *Macbeth,* which do not move us to nervous laughter:

> For brave Macbeth (well he deserves that name),
> Disdaining Fortune, with his brandish'd steel,
> Which smok'd with bloody execution,
> Like Valour's minion, carv'd out his passage,
> Till he fac'd the slave;
> Which ne'er shook hands, nor bade farewell to him,
> Till he unseam'd him from the nave to th' chops,
> And fix'd his head upon our battlements.
>
> [I.ii. 16–23]

I cannot recall anyone else in Shakespeare who sustains a death wound from the navel all the way up to his jaw, a mode of unseaming that introduces us to Macbeth's quite astonishing ferocity. "Bellona's bridegroom," Macbeth is thus the husband to the war goddess, and his unseaming strokes enact his husbandly function. Devoted as he and Lady Macbeth palpably are to each other, their love has its problematic elements. Shakespeare's sources gave him a Lady Macbeth previously married, and presumably grieving for a dead son by that marriage. The mutual passion between her and Macbeth depends upon their dream of a shared "greatness," the promise of which seems to have been an element in Macbeth's courtship, since she reminds him of it when he wavers. Her power over him, with its angry questioning of his manliness, is engendered by her evident frustration—certainly of ambition, manifestly of motherhood, possibly also of sexual fulfillment. Victor Hugo, when he placed Macbeth in the line of Nimrod, the Bible's first "hunter of men," may have hinted that few of them have been famous as lovers. Macbeth sees himself always as a soldier, therefore not cruel but professionally murderous, which allows him to maintain also a curious, personal passivity, almost more the dream than the dreamer. Famously a paragon of courage and so no coward, Macbeth nevertheless is in a perpetual state of fear. Of what? Part of the answer seems to be his fear of impotence, a dread related as much to his overwhelming power of imagination as to his shared dream of greatness with Lady Macbeth.

Critics almost always find an element of sexual violence in Macbeth's murder of the sleeping and benign Duncan. Macbeth himself overdetermines this critical discovery when he compares his movement toward the murder with "Tarquin's ravishing strides" on that tyrant's way to rape the chaste Lucrece, heroine of Shakespeare's poem. Is this a rare, self-referential moment on Shakespeare's own part, since many in Macbeth's audience would have recognized the dramatist's reference to one of his nondramatic works, which was more celebrated in Shakespeare's time than it is in ours? If it is, then Shakespeare brings his imagination very close to Macbeth's in the moment just preceding his protagonist's initial crime. Think how many are murdered onstage in Shakespeare, and reflect why we are not allowed to watch Macbeth's stabbings of Duncan. The unseen nature of the butchery allows us to imagine, rather horribly, the location and number of Macbeth's thrusts into the sleeping body of the man who is at once his cousin, his guest, his king, and symbolically his benign father. I assumed that, in *Julius Caesar*, Brutus's thrust was at Caesar's privates, enhancing the horror of the tradition that Brutus was Caesar's natural son. The corpse of Duncan is described by Macbeth in accents that remind us of Antony's account of the murdered Caesar, yet there is something more intimate in Macbeth's phrasing:

> Here lay Duncan,
> His silver skin lac'd with his golden blood;
> And his gash'd stabs look'd like a breach in nature
> For ruin's wasteful entrance.
>
> > [II.iii.111–14]

Macbeth and "ruin" are one, and the sexual suggestiveness in "breach in nature" and "wasteful entrance" is very strong, and counterpoints itself against Lady Macbeth's bitter reproaches at Macbeth's refusal to return with the daggers, which would involve his seeing the corpse again. "Infirm of purpose!" she cries out to him first, and when she returns from planting the daggers, her imputation of his sexual failure is more overt: "Your constancy/Hath left you unattended," another reminder that his firmness has abandoned him. But perhaps desire, except to perpetuate himself in time, has departed forever from him. He has doomed himself to be the "poor player," an overanxious actor always missing his cues. Iago and Edmund, in somewhat diverse

ways, were both playwrights staging their own works, until Iago
was unmasked by Emilia and Edmund received his death wound
from the nameless knight, Edgar's disguise. Though Iago and
Edmund also played brilliantly in their self-devised roles, they
showed their genius primarily as plotters. Macbeth plots inces-
santly, but cannot make the drama go as he wishes. He botches
it perpetually, and grows more and more outraged that his
bloodiest ideas, when accomplished, trail behind them a residuum
that threatens him still. Malcolm and Donalbain, Fleance and
Macduff—all flee, and their survival is for Macbeth the stuff of
nightmare.

Nightmare seeks Macbeth out; that search, more than his violence, is the true plot of this most terrifying of Shakespeare's
plays. From my childhood on, I have been puzzled by the Witches,
who spur the rapt Macbeth on to his sublime but guilty project.
They come to him because preternaturally they *know* him: he is
not so much theirs as they are his. This is not to deny their reality apart from him, but only to indicate again that he has more
implicit power over them than they manifest in regard to him.
They place nothing in his mind that is not already there. And yet
they undoubtedly influence his total yielding to his own ambitious imagination. Perhaps, indeed, they are the final impetus that
renders Macbeth so ambiguously passive when he confronts the
phantasmagorias that Lady Macbeth says always have attended
him. In that sense, the Weird Sisters are close to the three Norns,
or Fates, that William Blake interpreted them as being: they gaze
into the seeds of time, but they also act upon those they teach to
gaze with them. Together with Lady Macbeth, they persuade
Macbeth to his self-abandonment, or rather they prepare Macbeth for Lady Macbeth's greater temptation into unsanctified
violence.

Surely the play inherits their cosmos, and not a Christian

universe. Hecate, goddess of spells, is the deity of the night world, and though she calls Macbeth "a wayward son," his actions pragmatically make him a loyal associate of the evil sorceress. One senses, in rereading *Macbeth,* a greater preternatural energy within Macbeth himself than is available to Hecate or to the Weird Sisters. Our equivocal but compulsive sympathy for him is partly founded upon Shakespeare's exclusion of any other human center of interest, except for his prematurely eclipsed wife, and partly upon our fear that his imagination is our own. Yet the largest element in our irrational sympathy ensues from Macbeth's sublimity. Great utterance continuously breaks through his confusions, and a force neither divine nor wicked seems to choose him as the trumpet of its prophecy:

> Besides, this Duncan
> Hath borne his faculties so meek, hath been
> So clear in his great office, that his virtues
> Will plead like angels, trumpet-tongu'd against
> The deep damnation of his taking-off;
> And Pity, like a naked new-born babe,
> Striding the blast, or heaven's Cherubins, hors'd
> Upon the sightless couriers of the air,
> Shall blow the horrid deed in every eye,
> That tears shall drown the wind.
>
> [I.vii. 16–25]

Here, as elsewhere, we do not feel that Macbeth's proleptic eloquence is inappropriate to him; his language and his imaginings are those of a seer, which heightens the horror of his disintegration into the bloodiest of all Shakespearean tyrant-villains. Yet we wonder just how and why this great voice breaks through Macbeth's consciousness, since clearly it comes to him unbidden.

He is, we know, given to seizures; Lady Macbeth remarks, "My Lord is often thus,/And hath been from his youth." Visionary fits come upon him when and as *they* will, and his tendency to second sight is clearly allied both to his proleptic imaginings and to the witches' preoccupation with him. No one else in Shakespeare is so occult, not even the hermetic magician, Prospero.

This produces an extraordinary effect upon us, since we *are* Macbeth, though we are pragmatically neither murderers nor mediums, and he is. Nor are we conduits for transcendent energies, for visions and voices; Macbeth is as much a natural poet as he is a natural killer. He cannot reason and compare, because images beyond reason and beyond competition overwhelm him. Shakespeare can be said to have conferred his own intellect upon Hamlet, his own capacity for more life upon Falstaff, his own wit upon Rosalind. To Macbeth, Shakespeare evidently gave over what might be called the passive element in his own imagination. We cannot judge that the author of *Macbeth* was victimized by his own imagination, but we hardly can avoid seeing Macbeth himself as the victim of a beyond that surmounts anything available to us. His tragic dignity depends upon his contagious sense of unknown modes of being, his awareness of powers that lie beyond Hecate and the witches but are not identical with the Christian God and His angels. These powers are the tragic sublime itself, and Macbeth, despite his own will, is so deeply at one with them that he can contaminate us with sublimity, even as the unknown forces contaminate him. Critics have never agreed as to how to name those forces; it seems to me best to agree with Nietzsche that the prejudices of morality are irrelevant to such daemons. If they terrify us by taking over this play, they also bring us joy, the utmost pleasure that accepts contamination by the daemonic.

5

Macbeth, partly because of this uncanniness, is fully the rival of *Hamlet* and of *King Lear,* and like them transcends what might seem the limits of art. Yet the play defies critical description and analysis in ways very different from those of *Hamlet* and *Lear.* Hamlet's inwardness is an abyss; Lear's sufferings finally seem more than human; Macbeth is all too human. Despite Macbeth's violence, he is much closer to us than are Hamlet and Lear. What makes this usurper so intimate for us? Even great actors do badly in the role, with only a few exceptions, Ian McKellen being much the best I've attended. Yet even McKellen seemed haunted by the precariousness of the role's openness to its audience. I think we most identify with Macbeth because we also have the sense that we are violating our own natures, as he does his. *Macbeth,* in another of Shakespeare's startling originalities, is the first Expressionist drama. The consciousness of Hamlet is wider than ours, but Macbeth's is not; it seems indeed to have exactly our contours, whoever we are. And as I have emphasized already, the proleptic element in Macbeth's imagination reaches out to our own apprehensiveness, our universal sense that the dreadful is about to happen, and that we have no choice but to participate in it.

When Malcolm, at the play's end, refers to "this dead butcher, and his fiend-like Queen," we are in the odd position both of having to agree with Duncan's son and of murmuring to ourselves that so to categorize Macbeth and Lady Macbeth seems scarcely adequate. Clearly the ironies of *Macbeth* are not born of clashing perspectives but of divisions in the self—in Macbeth and in the audience. When Macbeth says that in him "function is smother'd in surmise," we have to agree, and then we brood on to what more limited extent this is true of ourselves also. Dr. Johnson said that in Macbeth "the events are too great to admit the influence of particular dispositions." Since no one feared more than Johnson what he called "the dangerous prevalence of the imagination," I have to assume that the greatest of all critics wished not to acknowledge that the particular disposition of Macbeth's proleptic imagination overdetermines the events of the play. Charting some of the utterances of this leaping-ahead in Macbeth's mind ought to help us to leap ahead in his wake.

In a rapt aside, quite early in the play, Macbeth introduces us to the extraordinary nature of his imagination:

> This supernatural soliciting
> Cannot be ill; cannot be good:—
> If ill, why hath it given me earnest of success,
> Commencing in a truth? I am Thane of Cawdor:
> If good, why do I yield to that suggestion
> Whose horrid image doth unfix my hair,
> And make my seated heart knock at my ribs,
> Against the use of nature? Present fears
> Are less than horrible imaginings.
> My thought, whose murther yet is but fantastical,
> Shakes so my single state of man
> That function is smother'd in surmise,
> And nothing is, but what is not.
>
> [I.iii. 130–42]

"My single state of man" plays upon several meanings of "single": unitary, isolated, vulnerable. The phantasmagoria of murdering Duncan is so vivid that "nothing is, but what is not," and "function," the mind, is smothered by "surmise," fantasy. The dramatic music of this passage, impossible not to discern with the inner ear, is very difficult to describe. Macbeth speaks to himself in a kind of trance, halfway between trauma and second sight.

An involuntary visionary of horror, he *sees* what certainly is going to happen, while still knowing this murder to be "but fantastical." His tribute to his own "horrible imaginings" is absolute: the implication is that his will is irrelevant. That he stands on the border of madness may seem evident to us now, but such a judgment would be mistaken. It is the resolute Lady Macbeth who goes mad; the proleptic Macbeth will become more and more outraged and outrageous, but he is no more insane at the close than he is here. The parameters of the diseased mind waver throughout Shakespeare. Is Hamlet ever truly mad, even north-by-northwest? Lear, Othello, Leontes, Timon all pass into derangement and (partly) out again, but Lady Macbeth is granted no recovery. It might be a relief for us if Macbeth ever went mad, but he cannot, if only because he represents all our imaginations, including our capacity for anticipating futures we both wish for and fear.

At his castle, with Duncan as his royal guest, Macbeth attempts a soliloquy in Hamlet's mode, but rapidly leaps into his own:

> If it were done, when 'tis done, then 'twere well
> It were done quickly: If th' assassination
> Could trammel up the consequence, and catch
> With his surcease, success; that but this blow
> Might be the be-all and the end-all—here,
> But here, upon this bank and shoal of time,
> We'd jump the life to come.
>
> [I.vii. 1–7]

"Jump" partly means "risk," but Shakespeare carries it over into our meaning also. After the great vision of "Pity, like a naked new-born babe" descends upon Macbeth from some transcendent realm, the usurping host has another fantasy concerning his own will:

I have no spur
To prick the sides of my intent, but only
Vaulting ambition, which o'erleaps itself
And falls on th' other—

[I.vii.25–28]

Lady Macbeth then enters, and so Macbeth does not complete his metaphor. "The other" what? Not "side," for his horse, which is all will, has had its sides spurred, so that ambition evidently is now on the other shoal or shore, its murder of Duncan established as a desire. That image is central in the play, and Shakespeare takes care to keep it phantasmagoric by not allowing us to see the actual murder of Duncan. On his way to this regicide, Macbeth has a vision that takes him even further into the realm where "nothing is, but what is not":

Is this a dagger, which I see before me,
The handle toward my hand? Come, let me clutch thee:—
I have thee not, and yet I see thee still.
Art thou not, fatal vision, sensible
To feeling, as to sight? or art thou but
A dagger of the mind, a false creation,
Proceeding from the heat-oppressed brain?
I see thee yet, in form as palpable
As this which now I draw.
Thou marshall'st me the way that I was going;
And such an instrument I was to use.—
Mine eyes are made the fools o' th' other senses,
Or else worth all the rest: I see thee still;
And on thy blade, and dudgeon, gouts of blood,
Which was not so before.—There's no such thing.
It is the bloody business which informs
Thus to mine eyes.—Now o'er the one half-world

Nature seems dead, and wicked dreams abuse
The curtain'd sleep: Witchcraft celebrates
Pale Hecate's off'rings; and wither'd Murther,
Alarum'd by his sentinel, the wolf,
Whose howl's his watch, thus with his stealthy pace,
With Tarquin's ravishing strides, towards his design
Moves like a ghost.——Thou sure and firm-set earth,
Hear not my steps, which way they walk, for fear
Thy very stones prate of my where-about,
And take the present horror from the time,
Which now suits with it.——Whiles I threat, he lives:
Words to the heat of deeds too cold breath gives.

A bell rings.

I go, and it is done: the bell invites me.
Hear it not, Duncan; for it is a knell
That summons thee to Heaven, or to Hell.

[II.i.33–64]

This magnificent soliloquy, culminating in the tolling of the
bell, always has been judged to be an apotheosis of Shakespeare's
art. So accustomed is Macbeth to second sight that he evidences
neither surprise nor fear at the visionary knife but coolly attempts to grasp this "dagger of the mind." The phrase "a false
creation" subtly hints at the gnostic cosmos of *Macbeth,* which is
the work of some Demiurge, whose botchings made creation itself a fall. With a wonderful metaphysical courage, admiration for
which helps implicate us in Macbeth's guilts, he responds to the
phantasmagoria by drawing his own dagger, thus acknowledging
his oneness with his own proleptic yearnings. As in *King Lear,*
the primary meaning of *fool* in this play is "victim," but Macbeth
defiantly asserts the possibility that his eyes, rather than being
victims, may be worth all his other senses together.

This moment of bravura is dispersed by a new phenomenon

in Macbeth's visionary history, as the hallucination undergoes a temporal transformation, great drops of blood manifesting themselves upon blade and handle. "There's no such thing," he attempts to insist, but yields instead to one of those openings-out of eloquence that perpetually descend upon him. In that yielding to Hecate's sorcery, Macbeth astonishingly identifies his steps toward the sleeping Duncan with Tarquin's "ravishing strides" toward his victim in Shakespeare's narrative poem *The Rape of Lucrece*. Macbeth is not going to ravish Duncan, except of his life, but the allusion would have thrilled many in the audience. I again take it that this audacity is Shakespeare's own signature, establishing his complicity with his protagonist's imagination. "I go, and it is done" constitutes the climactic prolepsis; we participate, feeling that Duncan is dead already, before the thrusts have been performed.

It is after the next murder, Banquo's, and after Macbeth's confrontation with Banquo's ghost, that the proleptic utterances begin to yield to the usurper's sense of being more outraged than outrageous:

Blood hath been shed ere now, i' th' olden time,
Ere humane statute purged the gentle weal;
Ay, and since too, murthers have been perform'd
Too terrible for the ear: the time has been,
That, when the brains were out, the man would die,
And there an end; but now, they rise again,
With twenty mortal murthers on their crowns,
And push us from our stools. This is more strange
Than such a murther is.

[III.iv.74–82]

Since moral contexts, as Nietzsche advised us, are simply irrelevant to *Macbeth,* its protagonist's increasing sense of outrage is perhaps not as outrageous as it should be. The witches equivocate with him, but they are rather equivocal entities in any case; I like Bradshaw's remark that they "seem curiously capricious and infantile, hardly less concerned with pilots and chestnuts than with Macbeth and Scotland." Far from governing the *kenoma,* or cosmological emptiness, in which *Macbeth* is set, they seem much punier components of it than Macbeth himself. A world that fell even as it was created is anything but a Christian nature. Though Hecate has some potency in this nature, one feels a greater Demiurgical force at loose in this play. Shakespeare will not name it, except to call it "time," but that is a highly metaphorical time, not the "olden time" or good old days, when you bashed someone's brains out and so ended them, but "now," when their ghosts displace us.

That "now" is the empty world of *Macbeth,* into which we, as audience, *have been thrown,* and that sense of "thrownness" *is* the terror that Wilbur Sanders and Graham Bradshaw emphasize in *Macbeth.* When Macduff has fled to England, Macbeth chills us with a vow: "From this moment,/The very firstlings of my heart shall be/The firstlings of my hand." Since those firstlings pledge the massacre of Lady Macduff, her children, and all "unfortunate souls" related to Macduff, we are to appreciate that the heart of Macbeth is very much also the heart of the play's world. Macbeth's beheading by Macduff prompts the revenger, at the end, to proclaim, "The time is free," but we do not believe Macduff. How can we? The world is Macbeth's, precisely as he imagined it; only the kingdom belongs to Malcolm. *King Lear,* also set in the cosmological emptiness, is too various to be typified by any single utterance, even of Lear's own, but Macbeth concentrates his play and his world in its most famous speech:

> She should have died hereafter:
> There would have been a time for such a word.—
> To-morrow, and to-morrow, and to-morrow,

Creeps in this petty pace from day to day,
To the last syllable of recorded time;
And all our yesterdays have lighted fools
The way to dusty death. Out, out, brief candle!
Life's but a walking shadow; a poor player,
That struts and frets his hour upon the stage,
And then is heard no more: it is a tale
Told by an idiot, full of sound and fury,
Signifying nothing.

[V.v.17–28]

Dr. Johnson, rightly shocked that this should be Macbeth's response to the death of his wife, at first insisted that "such a word" was an error for "such a world." When the Grand Cham retreated from this emendation, he stubbornly argued that "word" meant "intelligence" in the sense of "information," and so did not refer to "hereafter," as, alas, it certainly does. Johnson's moral genius was affronted, as it was by the end of *King Lear,* and Johnson was right: neither play sees with Christian optics. Macbeth has the authority to speak for his play and his world, as for his self. In Macbeth's time there is no hereafter, in any world. And yet this is the suicide of his own wife that has been just reported to him. Grief, in any sense we could apprehend, is not expressed by him. Instead of an elegy for Queen Macbeth, we hear a nihilistic death march, or rather a creeping of fools, of universal victims. The "brief candle" is both the sun and the individual life, no longer the "great bond" of Macbeth's magnificent invocation just before Banquo's murder:

Come, seeling night,
Scarf up the tender eye of pitiful Day,
And, with thy bloody and invisible hand,

Cancel, and tear to pieces, that great bond
Which keeps me pale!—Light thickens; and the crow
Makes wing to th' rooky wood;
Good things of Day begin to droop and drowse,
Whiles Night's black agents to their preys do rouse.
Thou marvell'st at my words: but hold thee still;
Things bad begun make strong themselves by ill.

[III.iii.46–55]

There the night becomes a royal falcon rending the sun
apart, and Macbeth's imagination is wholly apocalyptic. In the
"To-morrow, and to-morrow, and to-morrow" chant, the tenor
is postapocalyptic, as it will be in Macbeth's reception of the
news that Birnam Wood has come to Dunsinane:

I 'gin to be aweary of the sun,
And wish th' estate o' th' world were now undone.—

[V.v.49–50]

Life is a walking shadow in that sun, a staged representation
like the bad actor whose hour of strutting and fretting will not
survive our leaving the theater. Having carried the reverberation
of Ralph Richardson as Falstaff in my ear for half a century, I
reflect (as Shakespeare, not Macbeth, meant me to reflect) that
Richardson will not be "heard no more" until I am dead. Macbeth's finest verbal coup is to revise his metaphor; life suddenly is
no longer a bad actor, but an idiot's story, nihilistic of necessity.
The magnificent language of Macbeth and of his play is reduced
to "sound and fury," but that phrase plays back against Macbeth,
his very diction, in all its splendor, refuting him. It is as though
he at last refuses himself any imaginative sympathy, a refusal
impossible for his audience to make.

6

I come back, for a last time, to the terrible awe that Macbeth provokes in us. G. Wilson Knight first juxtaposed a reflection by Lafew, the wise old nobleman of *All's Well That Ends Well,* with *Macbeth*:

> *Laf*. They say miracles are past; and we have our philosophical persons to make modern and familiar, things supernatural and causeless. Hence is it that we make trifles of terrors, ensconcing ourselves into seeming knowledge, when we should submit ourselves to an unknown fear.
>
> [II.iii.1–6]

Wilbur Sanders, acknowledging Wilson Knight, explores *Macbeth* as the Shakespearean play where most we "submit ourselves to an unknown fear." My own experience of the play is that we rightly react to it with terror, even as we respond to *Hamlet* with wonder. Whatever *Macbeth* does otherwise, it certainly does not offer us a catharsis for the terrors it evokes. Since we are compelled to internalize Macbeth, the "unknown fear" finally is of ourselves. If we submit to it—and Shakespeare gives us little choice—then we follow Macbeth into a nihilism very different from the abyss-voyages of Iago and of Edmund. They are confident nihilists, secure in their self-election. Macbeth is never secure, nor are we, his unwilling cohorts; he childers, as we father, and we are the only children he has.

The most surprising observation on fear in *Macbeth* was also Wilson Knight's:

> Whilst Macbeth lives in conflict with himself there is misery, evil, fear; when, at the end, he and others have openly

identified himself with evil, he faces the world fearless: nor does he appear evil any longer.

I think I see where Wilson Knight was aiming, but a few revisions are necessary. Macbeth's broad progress is from proleptic horror to a sense of baffled expectations, in which a feeling of having been outraged takes the place of fear. "Evil" we can set aside; it is redundant, rather like calling Hitler or Stalin evil. When Macbeth is betrayed, by hallucination and foretelling, he manifests a profound and energetic outrage, like a frantic actor always fated to miss all his cues. The usurper goes on murdering, and achieves no victory over time or the self. Sometimes I wonder whether Shakespeare somehow had gotten access to the Gnostic and Manichaean fragments scattered throughout the Church Fathers, quoted by them only to be denounced, though I rather doubt that Shakespeare favored much ecclesiastical reading. Macbeth, however intensely we identify with him, is more frightening than anything he confronts, thus intimating that we ourselves may be more dreadful than anything in our own worlds. And yet Macbeth's realm, like ours, can be a ghastly context:

Old Man. Threescore and ten I can remember well;
    Within the volume of which time I have seen
    Hours dreadful, and things strange, but this sore night
    Hath trifled former knowings.
Rosse.   Ha, good Father,
    Thou seest the heavens, as troubled with man's act,
    Threatens his bloody stage: by th' clock 'tis day,
    And yet dark night strangles the travelling lamp.
    Is 't night's predominance, or the day's shame,
    That darkness does the face of earth entomb,
    When living light should kiss it?

Old Man.   'Tis unnatural,
   Even like the deed that's done. On Tuesday last,
   A falcon, towering in her pride of place,
   Was by a mousing owl hawk'd at and kill'd.
Rosse. And Duncan's horses (a thing most strange and
   certain)
   Beauteous and swift, the minions of their race,
   Turn'd wild in nature, broke their stalls, flung out,
   Contending 'gainst obedience, as they would make
   War with mankind.
Old Man.   'Tis said, they eat each other.
Rosse. They did so; to th' amazement of mine eyes,
   That look'd upon 't.

                                                      [II.iv.1–20]

This is the aftermath of Duncan's murder, yet even at the play's opening a wounded captain admiringly says of Macbeth and Banquo: "they/Doubly redoubled strokes upon the foe:/Except they meant to bathe in reeking wounds,/Or memorize another Golgotha,/I cannot tell—." What does it mean to "memorize another Golgotha"? Golgotha, "the place of skulls," was Calvary, where Jesus suffered upon the cross. "Memorize" here seems to mean "memorialize," and Shakespeare subtly has invoked a shocking parallel. We are at the beginning of the play, and these are still the *good* captains Macbeth and Banquo, patriotically fighting for Duncan and for Scotland, yet they are creating a new slaughter ground for a new Crucifixion. Graham Bradshaw aptly has described the horror of nature in *Macbeth,* and Robert Watson has pointed to its gnostic affinities. Shakespeare throws us into everything that is not ourselves, not so as to induce an ascetic revulsion in the audience, but so as to compel a choice between Macbeth and the cosmological emptiness, the *kenoma* of the Gnostics. We choose Macbeth perforce, and the preference is made very costly for us.

Of the aesthetic greatness of *Macbeth,* there can be no question. The play cannot challenge the scope and depth of *Hamlet* and *King Lear,* or the brilliant painfulness of *Othello,* or the world-without-end panorama of *Antony and Cleopatra,* and yet it is my personal favorite of all the high tragedies. Shakespeare's final strength is radical internalization, and this is his most internalized drama, played out in the guilty imagination that we share with Macbeth. No critical method that works equally well for Thomas Middleton or John Fletcher and for Shakespeare is going to illuminate Shakespeare for us. I do not know whether God created Shakespeare, but I know that Shakespeare created us, to an altogether startling degree. In relation to us, his perpetual audience, Shakespeare is a kind of mortal god; our instruments for measuring him break when we seek to apply them. *Macbeth,* as its best critics have seen, scarcely shows us that crimes against nature are repaired when a legitimate social order is restored. Nature *is* crime in *Macbeth,* but hardly in the Christian sense that calls out for nature to be redeemed by grace, or by expiation and forgiveness. As in *King Lear,* we have no place to go in *Macbeth;* there is no sanctuary available to us. Macbeth himself exceeds us, in energy and in torment, but he also represents us, and we discover him more vividly within us the more deeply we delve.

william shakespeare
macbeth

synopsis

In the midst of thunder and lightning on a barren Scottish heath crouch three uncanny witches in wild attire waiting to intercept the two successful generals, Macbeth and Banquo, on their return from battle where they have just quelled a rebellion led by the traitorous thane of Cawdor against the gentle, unwarlike King Duncan. The witches hail Macbeth first with his own title, thane of Glamis, then as thane of Cawdor, then as "King hereafter." Banquo quickly remarks Macbeth's sudden start at the witches' words, then asks for a prophecy for himself and is told that he will beget kings though he is not one. Macbeth is profoundly stirred when part of the prophecy is fulfilled a few minutes later, two noblemen sent by the King greeting him with the title of the thane of Cawdor who has been put to death. As Duncan's sons are young, Macbeth being the King's cousin had hoped to succeed him in accordance with the Scottish law but the old King announces to his thanes that his eldest son Malcolm will henceforth be known as Duke of Cumberland, heir to the throne.

Macbeth's slumbering ambitions become determined and malignant, and murderous thoughts surge through his brain when Duncan signifies his desire to remain overnight with his sons at Macbeth's castle. Lady Macbeth, as a devoted loving wife, shares her husband's ambitions but, knowing he is not hardened in wickedness, mistrusts his courage and resoluteness, and she herself makes a daring brutal plot against the King's life which she forces her vacillating husband to accept.

The two grooms of the King's bedchamber are soundly drugged, Macbeth stabs the sleeping Duncan to death, and Lady Macbeth finishes the awful night's work by smearing the unconscious grooms with blood and laying their reeking daggers beside them. In the morning when the murder is discovered, Macbeth affects great grief and to show his indignation he kills the King's grooms whom he declares are the assassins. The princes, knowing their personal danger and having few doubts as to the real murderer, keep discreet silence and flee the country, Malcolm going to England and Donalbain to Ireland, whereupon Macbeth insinuates that they are the originators of the crime.

Although he now is the crowned King of Scotland, Macbeth remains unsatisfied, knowing that Banquo suspects him of Duncan's murder and galled by the remembrance of the witches' prophecy that another man's children will be kings. No longer wavering and hesitant, he promptly accomplishes the murder of Banquo on the same night when he is giving a formal banquet to his thanes. While he is praising Banquo and pretending to regret his absence, the murdered man's ghost enters the banquet hall and takes his vacant seat at the table, unseen by all but Macbeth who utters such words of terrified guilt that the noblemen are both confused and suspicious, and Lady Macbeth hurriedly breaks up the gathering.

Frustrated in his plans by the escape of Fleance, Banquo's son, from the murderers, Macbeth visits the witches' cavern, where

Hecate, Queen of Evil, has plotted his downfall, and the witches make revelations in which the truth is disguised, mysterious and misleading. They warn him against Macduff, a powerful thane, by showing him an armed head; the apparition of a bloody child bids him be bold and resolute, for no one born of woman will harm him; and a crowned child follows with a tree in his hand, telling him to be lion-hearted and brave for he will never be vanquished until Birnam Wood, near his castle at Dunsinane, moves against him. Although he is afterwards tormented by the sight of eight kings accompanied by Banquo's ghost who smilingly points to them as his progeny, Macbeth pins his faith in the witches' prophecies, places spies in all the thanes' houses to watch their movements, and comes to be feared and hated as a tyrant. When news reaches him of Macduff's flight to England to join Malcolm who is preparing to recover the throne of Scotland, he orders the slaughter of the thane's helpless wife and little children.

Meanwhile in his castle, Lady Macbeth, her mind deranged by its hideous memories, walks and talks piteously in her sleep, revealing their dreadful crimes, and the kindly doctor assures her husband that medicines will not help her. But Macbeth has little time to give her as he is busily preparing to meet the advancing English army under Malcolm and Siward, Lord of Northumberland, who have combined with some rebellious Scottish forces near Birnam Wood. To conceal their numbers, Malcolm orders each soldier to carry before him a leafy branch, with the result that a white-faced, trembling servant rushes into Macbeth's presence with the news that Birnam Wood is moving! At the same time a messenger brings tidings of Lady Macbeth's death.

The desperate, raging King, battling with all his tremendous energy in a losing fight, his soldiers deserting him by scores, encounters young Siward, the English general's son, who fights him upon hearing his hated name, and is killed. Still muttering the prophetic words that no one born of woman will harm him, Macbeth is suddenly faced with Macduff, thirsting for revenge, who scoffs at the witches' charm by saying that he himself was born untimely, and taunts his enemy by declaring that his head will soon be placed on a pole for the public gaze. Macbeth falls fighting, and Macduff hails the victorious Malcolm at Dunsinane castle with the tyrant's head.

historical data

The chief source of the story of *Macbeth* is *The Chronicle of England and Scotland* by Holinshed published in 1577 which in turn was founded largely on the *Scotorum Historia* of Hector Boece (1526). The earliest source of this material probably came from the Scottish historians, John of Fordun (1360) and Andrew of Wyntoun (1420). There is, however, a great deal of purely legendary matter in all of these accounts. The scene is laid in about the year 1040 and recent opinion is indicated that the legendary *Macbeth* was a rather more worthy monarch than the character created by Shakespeare.

Shakespeare added many incidents to the bare details of the earlier accounts. Banquo's ghost, the porter scene, the sleep-walking scene and the famous soliloquies appear to have had no prototype in the earlier works.

There may, perhaps, have been in existence an earlier play on this subject which is not extant, for there was entered for registration in the Stationers' Register in 1596 a ballad or stage play (?) entitled *Macdobeth*.

From political allusions, a reference to the practice of touching for the King's evil which James I was induced to revive, and minor indications in the text, the date of composition of *Macbeth* is generally fixed as 1606. It was first published in the First Folio in 1623.

dramatis personæ

Duncan, *King of Scotland.*

Malcolm,
Donalbain, } *his sons.*

Macbeth,
Banquo, } *generals of the King's army.*

Macduff,
Lennox,
Ross,
Menteith, } *noblemen of Scotland.*
Angus,
Caithness,

Fleance, *son to Banquo.*

Siward, *earl of Northumberland, general of the English forces.*

Young Siward, *his son.*

Seyton, *an officer attending on Macbeth.*

Boy, *son to Macduff.*

An English Doctor.

A Scotch Doctor.

A Sergeant.

A Porter.

An Old Man.

Lady Macbeth.

Lady Macduff.

Gentlewoman *attending on Lady Macbeth.*

Hecate.

Three Witches.

Apparitions.

Lords, Gentlemen, Officers, Soldiers, Murderers, Attendants, and
Messengers.

Scene: Scotland; England.

act 1

scene 1. [*A desert place*]

Thunder and lightning. Enter Three Witches

First Witch. When shall we three meet again?
  In thunder, lightning, or in rain?

Second Witch. When the hurlyburly's done,
  When the battle's lost and won.

Third Witch. That will be ere the set of sun.

First Witch. Where the place?

Second Witch.   Upon the heath.

Third Witch. There to meet with Macbeth.

First Witch. I come, Graymalkin.

Second Witch. Paddock calls:—anon!

All. Fair is foul, and foul is fair.
  Hover through the fog and filthy air.

                                                    Exeunt.

scene 2. [*A camp near Forres*]

Alarum within. Enter Duncan, Malcolm, Donalbain,
Lennox, *with* Attendants, *meeting a bleeding* Sergeant

Duncan. What bloody man is that? He can report,
  As seemeth by his plight, of the revolt
  The newest state.

Malcolm.   This is the sergeant
  Who like a good and hardy soldier fought
  'Gainst my captivity. Hail, brave friend!
  Say to the king the knowledge of the broil
  As thou didst leave it.

Sergeant.   Doubtful it stood;
  As two spent swimmers, that do cling together
  And choke their art. The merciless Macdonwald—
  Worthy to be a rebel, for to that
  The multiplying villanies of nature
  Do swarm upon him—from the western isles
  Of kerns and gallowglasses is supplied;
  And Fortune, on his damned quarrel smiling,
  Show'd like a rebel's whore: but all's too weak:
  For brave Macbeth—well he deserves that name—
  Disdaining Fortune, with his brandish'd steel,
  Which smoked with bloody execution,
  Like valour's minion carved out his passage
  Till he faced the slave;
  Which ne'er shook hands, nor bade farewell to him,
  Till he unseam'd him from the nave to the chops,
  And fix'd his head upon our battlements.

Duncan. O valiant cousin! worthy gentleman!

Sergeant. As whence the sun 'gins his reflection
    Shipwracking storms and direful thunders break,
    So from that spring whence comfort seem'd to come
    Discomfort swells. Mark, king of Scotland, mark:
    No sooner justice had, with valour arm'd,
    Compell'd these skipping kerns to trust their heels,
    But the Norweyan lord, surveying vantage,
    With furbish'd arms and new supplies of men,
    Began a fresh assault.

Duncan.   Dismay'd not this
    Our captains, Macbeth and Banquo?

Sergeant.   Yes;
    As sparrows eagles, or the hare the lion.
    If I say sooth, I must report they were
    As cannons overcharged with double cracks;
    So they
    Doubly redoubled strokes upon the foe:
    Except they meant to bathe in reeking wounds,
    Or memorize another Golgotha,
    I cannot tell—
    But I am faint; my gashes cry for help.

Duncan. So well thy words become thee as thy wounds;
    They smack of honour both. Go get him surgeons.

                            Exit Sergeant, *attended.*
    Who comes here?

               Enter Ross *and* Angus

Malcolm.   The worthy thane of Ross.

Lennox. What a haste looks through his eyes! So should he look
    That seems to speak things strange.

Ross.   God save the king!

Duncan. Whence cam'st thou, worthy thane?

Ross.   From Fife, great king;
   Where the Norweyan banners flout the sky
   And fan our people cold.
   Norway himself, with terrible numbers,
   Assisted by that most disloyal traitor
   The thane of Cawdor, began a dismal conflict;
   Till that Bellona's bridegroom, lapp'd in proof,
   Confronted him with self-comparisons,
   Point against point, rebellious arm 'gainst arm,
   Curbing his lavish spirit: and, to conclude,
   The victory fell on us.

Duncan.   Great happiness!

Ross. That now
   Sweno, the Norways' king, craves composition;
   Nor would we deign him burial of his men
   Till he disbursed, at Saint Colme's Inch,
   Ten thousand dollars to our general use.

Duncan. No more that thane of Cawdor shall deceive
   Our bosom interest: go pronounce his present death,
   And with his former title greet Macbeth.

Ross. I'll see it done.

Duncan. What he hath lost, noble Macbeth hath won.

                                            Exeunt.

scene 3.   [*A heath*]

Thunder. Enter the Three Witches

First Witch. Where hast thou been, sister?

Second Witch. Killing swine.

Third Witch. Sister, where thou?

First Witch. A sailor's wife had chestnuts in her lap,
    And mounch'd, and mounch'd, and mounch'd.
    'Give me,' quoth I:
    'Aroint thee, witch!' the rump-fed ronyon cries.
    Her husband's to Aleppo gone, master o' the *Tiger:*
    But in a sieve I'll thither sail,
    And, like a rat without a tail,
    I'll do, I'll do, and I'll do.

Second Witch. I'll give thee a wind.

First Witch. Thou'rt kind.

Third Witch. And I another.

First Witch. I myself have all the other;
    And the very ports they blow,
    All the quarters that they know
    I' the shipman's card.
    I will drain him dry as hay:
    Sleep shall neither night nor day
    Hang upon his pent-house lid;
    He shall live a man forbid:
    Weary sev'nnights nine times nine
    Shall he dwindle, peak, and pine:
    Though his bark cannot be lost,
    Yet it shall be tempest-tost.
    Look what I have.

Second Witch. Show me, show me.

First Witch. Here I have a pilot's thumb,
    Wrack'd as homeward he did come.

                                Drum within.

Third Witch. A drum, a drum!
    Macbeth doth come.

All. The weïrd sisters, hand in hand,
   Posters of the sea and land,
   Thus do go about, about:
   Thrice to thine, and thrice to mine,
   And thrice again, to make up nine.
   Peace! the charm's wound up.
                 Enter Macbeth *and* Banquo

Macbeth. So foul and fair a day I have not seen.

Banquo. How far is 't call'd to Forres? What are these,
   So wither'd and so wild in their attire,
   That look not like the inhabitants o' the earth,
   And yet are on 't? Live you? or are you aught
   That man may question? You seem to understand me,
   By each at once her choppy finger laying
   Upon her skinny lips: you should be women,
   And yet your beards forbid me to interpet
   That you are so.

Macbeth.   Speak, if you can: what are you?

First Witch. All hail, Macbeth! hail to thee, thane of Glamis!

Second Witch. All hail, Macbeth! hail to thee, thane of Cawdor!

Third Witch. All hail, Macbeth, that shalt be king hereafter!

Banquo. Good sir, why do you start, and seem to fear
   Things that do sound so fair? I' the name of truth,
   Are ye fantastical, or that indeed
   Which outwardly ye show? My noble partner
   You greet with present grace and great prediction
   Of noble having and of royal hope,
   That he seems rapt withal: to me you speak not:
   If you can look into the seeds of time,
   And say which grain will grow and which will not,

Speak then to me, who neither beg nor fear
  Your favours nor your hate.

First Witch. Hail!

Second Witch. Hail!

Third Witch. Hail!

First Witch. Lesser than Macbeth, and greater.

Second Witch. Not so happy, yet much happier.

Third Witch. Thou shalt get kings, though thou be none:
  So all hail, Macbeth and Banquo!

First Witch. Banquo and Macbeth, all hail!

Macbeth. Stay, you imperfect speakers, tell me more:
  By Sinel's death I know I am thane of Glamis;
  But how of Cawdor? the thane of Cawdor lives,
  A prosperous gentleman; and to be king
  Stands not within the prospect of belief,
  No more than to be Cawdor. Say from whence
  You owe this strange intelligence? or why
  Upon this blasted heath you stop our way
  With such prophetic greeting? Speak, I charge you.
                             Witches *vanish*.

Banquo. The earth hath bubbles as the water has,
  And these are of them: whither are they vanish'd?

Macbeth. Into the air, and what seem'd corporal
  Melted as breath into the wind. Would they had stay'd!

Banquo. Were such things here as we do speak about?
  Or have we eaten on the insane root
  That takes the reason prisoner?

Macbeth. Your children shall be kings.

Banquo.   You shall be king.

Macbeth. And thane of Cawdor too: went it not so?

Banquo. To the selfsame tune and words. Who's here?

Enter Ross *and* Angus

Ross. The king hath happily received, Macbeth,
    The news of thy success: and when he reads
    Thy personal venture in the rebels' fight,
    His wonders and his praises do contend
    Which should be thine or his: silenced with that,
    In viewing o'er the rest o' the selfsame day,
    He finds thee in the stout Norweyan ranks,
    Nothing afeard of what thyself didst make,
    Strange images of death. As thick as hail
    Came post with post, and every one did bear
    Thy praises in his kingdom's great defence,
    And pour'd them down before him.

Angus.   We are sent
    To give thee, from our royal master, thanks;
    Only to herald thee into his sight,
    Not pay thee.

Ross. And for an earnest of a greater honour,
    He bade me, from him, call thee thane of Cawdor:
    In which addition, hail, most worthy thane!
    For it is thine.

Banquo.   What, can the devil speak true?

Macbeth. The thane of Cawdor lives: why do you dress me
    In borrow'd robes?

Angus.   Who was the thane lives yet,
    But under heavy judgement bears that life
    Which he deserves to lose. Whether he was combined
    With those of Norway, or did line the rebel
    With hidden help and vantage, or that with both
    He labour'd in his country's wrack, I know not;

But treasons capital, confess'd and proved,
Have overthrown him.

Macbeth. [*Aside*] Glamis, and thane of Cawdor:
The greatest is behind.—Thanks for your pains.—
Do you not hope your children shall be kings,
When those that gave the thane of Cawdor to me
Promised no less to them?

Banquo. That, trusted home,
Might yet enkindle you unto the crown,
Besides the thane of Cawdor. But 'tis strange:
And oftentimes, to win us to our harm,
The instruments of darkness tell us truths,
Win us with honest trifles, to betray's
In deepest consequence.
Cousins, a word, I pray you.

Macbeth. [*Aside*] Two truths are told,
As happy prologues to the swelling act
Of the imperial theme.—I thank you, gentlemen.—
[*Aside*] This supernatural soliciting
Cannot be ill; cannot be good: if ill,
Why hath it given me earnest of success,
Commencing in a truth? I am thane of Cawdor:
If good, why do I yield to that suggestion
Whose horrid image doth unfix my hair
And make my seated heart knock at my ribs,
Against the use of nature? Present fears
Are less than horrible imaginings:
My thought, whose murder yet is but fantastical,
Shakes so my single state of man that function
Is smother'd in surmise, and nothing is
But what is not.

Banquo. Look, how our partner's rapt.

Macbeth. [*Aside*] If chance will have me king, why, chance
may crown me,
Without my stir.

Banquo.   New honours come upon him,
Like our strange garments, cleave not to their mould
But with the aid of use.

Macbeth.   [*Aside*] Come what come may,
Time and the hour runs through the roughest day.

Banquo. Worthy Macbeth, we stay upon your leisure.

Macbeth. Give me your favour: my dull brain was wrought
With things forgotten. Kind gentlemen, your pains
Are register'd where every day I turn
The leaf to read them. Let us toward the king.
[*To Banquo*] Think upon what hath chanced, and at more
time,
The interim having weigh'd it, let us speak
Our free hearts each to other.

Banquo.   Very gladly.

Macbeth. Till then, enough. Come, friends.

                                        Exeunt.

scene 4.   [*Forres. The palace*]

Flourish. Enter Duncan, Malcolm, Donalbain,
Lennox, *and* Attendants

Duncan. Is execution done on Cawdor? Or not
Those in commission yet return'd?

Malcolm.   My liege,
They are not yet come back. But I have spoke
With one that saw him die, who did report

That very frankly he confess'd his treasons,
Implored your highness' pardon and set forth
A deep repentance: nothing in his life
Became him like the leaving it; he died
As one that had been studied in his death,
To throw away the dearest thing he owed
As 'twere a careless trifle.

Duncan.   There's no art
To find the mind's construction in the face:
He was a gentleman on whom I built
An absolute trust.
         Enter Macbeth, Banquo, Ross, *and* Angus
            O worthiest cousin!
The sin of my ingratitude even now
Was heavy on me: thou art so far before,
That swiftest wing of recompense is slow
To overtake thee. Would thou hadst less deserved,
That the proportion both of thanks and payment
Might have been mine! only I have left to say,
More is thy due than more than all can pay.

Macbeth. The service and the loyalty I owe,
In doing it, pays itself. Your highness' part
Is to receive our duties: and our duties
Are to your throne and state children and servants;
Which do but what they should, by doing every thing
Safe toward your love and honour.

Duncan.   Welcome hither:
I have begun to plant thee, and will labour
To make thee full of growing. Noble Banquo,
That hast no less deserved, nor must be known
No less to have done so: let me infold thee
And hold thee to my heart.

Banquo.   There if I grow,
    The harvest is your own.

Duncan.   My plenteous joys,
    Wanton in fulness, seek to hide themselves
    In drops of sorrow. Sons, kinsmen, thanes,
    And you whose places are the nearest, know,
    We will establish our estate upon
    Our eldest, Malcolm, whom we name hereafter
    The Prince of Cumberland: which honour must
    Not unaccompanied invest him only,
    But signs of nobleness, like stars, shall shine
    On all deservers. From hence to Inverness,
    And bind us further to you.

Macbeth. The rest is labour, which is not used for you:
    I'll be myself the harbinger, and make joyful
    The hearing of my wife with your approach;
    So humbly take my leave.

Duncan.   My worthy Cawdor!

Macbeth. [*Aside*] The Prince of Cumberland! that is a step
    On which I must fall down, or else o'erleap,
    For in my way it lies. Stars, hide your fires;
    Let not light see my black and deep desires:
    The eye wink at the hand; yet let that be
    Which the eye fears, when it is done, to see.

                                              Exit.

Duncan. True, worthy Banquo; he is full so valiant,
    And in his commendations I am fed;
    It is a banquet to me. Let's after him,
    Whose care is gone before to bid us welcome:
    It is a peerless kinsman.

                            Flourish. Exeunt.

scene 5.   [*Inverness.* Macbeth's *castle*]

Enter Lady Macbeth, *reading a letter*

Lady Macbeth. 'They met me in the day of success; and I have
   learned by the perfectest report, they have more in them than
   mortal knowledge. When I burned in desire to question
   them further, they made themselves air, into which they
   vanished. Whiles I stood rapt in the wonder of it, came mis-
   sives from the king, who all-hailed me "Thane of Cawdor;"
   by which title, before, these weïrd sisters saluted me, and
   referred me to the coming on of time, with "Hail, king that
   shalt be!" This have I thought good to deliver thee, my dearest
   partner of greatness, that thou mightst not lose the dues of
   rejoicing, by being ignorant of what greatness is promised
   thee. Lay it to thy heart, and farewell.'

Glamis thou art, and Cawdor, and shalt be
What thou art promised: yet do I fear thy nature;
It is too full o' the milk of human kindness
To catch the nearest way: thou wouldst be great;
Art not without ambition, but without
The illness should attend it: what thou wouldst highly,
That wouldst thou holily; wouldst not play false,
And yet wouldst strongly win: thou'ldst have, great Glamis,
That which cries 'Thus thou must do,' if thou have it;
And that which rather thou dost fear to do
Than wishest should be undone. Hie thee hither,
That I may pour my spirits in thine ear,
And chastise with the valour of my tongue
All that impedes thee from the golden round,

Which fate and metaphysical aid doth seem
To have thee crown'd withal.

Enter a Messenger

What is your tidings?

Messenger. The king comes here to-night.

Lady Macbeth.   Thou'rt mad to say it:
Is not thy master with him? who, were't so,
Would have inform'd for preparation.

Messenger. So please you, it is true: our thane is coming:
One of my fellows had the speed of him,
Who, almost dead for breath, had scarcely more
Than would make up his message.

Lady Macbeth.   Give him tending;
He brings great news.

Exit Messenger.

The raven himself is hoarse

That croaks the fatal entrance of Duncan
Under my battlements. Come, you spirits
That tend on mortal thoughts, unsex me here,
And fill me, from the crown to the toe, top-full
Of direst cruelty! make thick my blood,
Stop up th' access and passage to remorse,
That no compunctious visitings of nature
Shake my fell purpose, nor keep peace between
Th' effect and it! Come to my woman's breasts,
And take my milk for gall, you murdering ministers,
Wherever in your sightless substances
You wait on nature's mischief! Come, thick night,
And pall thee in the dunnest smoke of hell,
That my keen knife see not the wound it makes,
Nor heaven peep through the blanket of the dark,
To cry 'Hold, hold!'

Enter Macbeth

Great Glamis! worthy Cawdor!
Greater than both, by the all-hail hereafter!
Thy letters have transported me beyond
This ignorant present, and I feel now
The future in the instant.

Macbeth.   My dearest love,
Duncan comes here to-night.

Lady Macbeth.   And when goes hence?

Macbeth. To-morrow, as he purposes.

Lady Macbeth.   O, never
Shall sun that morrow see!
Your face, my thane, is as a book where men
May read strange matters. To beguile the time,
Look like the time; bear welcome in your eye,
Your hand, your tongue: look like the innocent flower,
But be the serpent under 't. He that's coming
Must be provided for: and you shall put
This night's great business into my dispatch;
Which shall to all our nights and days to come
Give solely sovereign sway and masterdom.

Macbeth. We will speak further.

Lady Macbeth.   Only look up clear;
To alter favour ever is to fear:
Leave all the rest to me.

                                        Exeunt.

scene 6. [*Before* Macbeth's *castle*]

Hautboys and torches. Enter Duncan, Malcolm, Donalbain,
Banquo, Lennox, Macduff, Ross, Angus, *and* Attendants

Duncan. This castle hath a pleasant seat; the air
    Nimbly and sweetly recommends itself
    Unto our gentle senses.

Banquo.   This guest of summer,
    The temple-haunting martlet, does approve
    By his loved mansionry that the heaven's breath
    Smells wooingly here: no jutty, frieze,
    Buttress, nor coign of vantage, but this bird
    Hath made his pendent bed and procreant cradle:
    Where they most breed and haunt, I have observed
    The air is delicate.

                Enter Lady Macbeth

Duncan.   See, see, our honour'd hostess!
    The love that follows us sometime is our trouble,
    Which still we thank as love. Herein I teach you
    How you shall bid God 'ild us for your pains,
    And thank us for your trouble.

Lady Macbeth.   All our service
    In every point twice done, and then done double,
    Were poor and single business to contend
    Against those honours deep and broad wherewith
    Your majesty loads our house: for those of old,
    And the late dignities heap'd up to them,
    We rest your hermits.

Duncan.   Where's the thane of Cawdor?
    We coursed him at the heels, and had a purpose

To be his purveyor: but he rides well,
And his great love, sharp as his spur, hath holp him
To his home before us. Fair and noble hostess,
We are your guest to-night.

Lady Macbeth.   Your servants ever
Have theirs, themselves, and what is theirs, in compt,
To make their audit at your highness' pleasure,
Still to return your own.

Duncan.   Give me your hand;
Conduct me to mine host: we love him highly,
And shall continue our graces towards him.
By your leave, hostess.

                                        Exeunt.

scene 7.   [Macbeth's *castle*]

Hautboys and torches. Enter a Sewer, *and divers*
Servants *with dishes and service, and pass over*
the stage. Then enter Macbeth

Macbeth. If it were done when 'tis done, then 'twere well
It were done quickly: if the assassination
Could trammel up the consequence, and catch
With his surcease, success; that but this blow
Might be the be-all and the end-all here,
But here, upon this bank and shoal of time,
We'd jump the life to come. But in these cases
We still have judgement here; that we but teach
Bloody instructions, which, being taught, return
To plague th' inventor: this even-handed justice
Commends th' ingredience of our poison'd chalice
To our own lips. He's here in double trust:

First, as I am his kinsman and his subject,
Strong both against the deed; then, as his host,
Who should against his murderer shut the door,
Not bear the knife myself. Besides, this Duncan
Hath borne his faculties so meek, hath been
So clear in his great office, that his virtues
Will plead like angels trumpet-tongued against
The deep damnation of his taking-off;
And Pity, like a naked new-born babe,
Striding the blast, or heaven's cherubin horsed
Upon the sightless couriers of the air,
Shall blow the horrid deed in every eye,
That tears shall drown the wind. I have no spur
To prick the sides of my intent, but only
Vaulting ambition, which o'erleaps itself
And falls on the other—

                Enter Lady Macbeth
                How now! what news?

Lady Macbeth. He has almost supp'd: why have you left the
    chamber?

Macbeth. Hath he ask'd for me?

Lady Macbeth.   Know you not he has?

Macbeth. We will proceed no further in this business:
    He hath honour'd me of late; and I have bought
    Golden opinions from all sorts of people,
    Which would be worn now in their newest gloss,
    Not cast aside so soon.

Lady Macbeth.   Was the hope drunk
    Wherein you dress'd yourself? hath it slept since?
    And wakes it now, to look so green and pale
    At what it did so freely? From this time
    Such I account thy love. Art thou afeard

To be the same in thine own act and valour
As thou art in desire? Wouldst thou have that
Which thou esteem'st the ornament of life,
And live a coward in thine own esteem,
Letting 'I dare not' wait upon 'I would,'
Like the poor cat i' the adage?

Macbeth.   Prithee, peace:
I dare do all that may become a man;
Who dares do more is none.

Lady Macbeth.   What beast was 't then
That made you break this enterprise to me?
When you durst do it, then you were a man;
And, to be more than what you were, you would
Be so much more the man. Nor time nor place
Did then adhere, and yet you would make both:
They have made themselves, and that their fitness now
Does unmake you. I have given suck, and know
How tender 'tis to love the babe that milks me:
I would, while it was smiling in my face,
Have pluck'd my nipple from his boneless gums,
And dash'd the brains out, had I so sworn as you
Have done to this.

Macbeth.   If we should fail?

Lady Macbeth.   We fail!
But screw your courage to the sticking-place,
And we'll not fail. When Duncan is asleep—
Whereto the rather shall his day's hard journey
Soundly invite him—his two chamberlains
Will I with wine and wassail so convince,
That memory, the warder of the brain,
Shall be a fume, and the receipt of reason
A limbec only: when in swinish sleep

Their drenched natures lie as in a death,
What cannot you and I perform upon
Th' unguarded Duncan? what not put upon
His spongy officers, who shall bear the guilt
Of our great quell?

Macbeth.　　　　　Bring forth men-children only;
For thy undaunted mettle should compose
Nothing but males. Will it not be received,
When we have mark'd with blood those sleepy two
Of his own chamber, and used their very daggers,
That they have done 't?

Lady Macbeth.　　　　Who dares receive it other,
As we shall make our griefs and clamour roar
Upon his death?

Macbeth.　　　　I am settled, and bend up
Each corporal agent to this terrible feat.
Away, and mock the time with fairest show:
False face must hide what the false heart doth know.

　　　　　　　　　　　　　　　　　　　Exeunt.

act 2

scene 1. [*Inverness. Court of* Macbeth's *castle*]

Enter Banquo, *and* Fleance *bearing a torch before him*

Banquo. How goes the night, boy?

Fleance. The moon is down; I have not heard the clock.

Banquo. And she goes down at twelve.

Fleance.   I take 't, 'tis later, sir.

Banquo. Hold, take my sword. There's husbandry in heaven,
   Their candles are all out. Take thee that too.
   A heavy summons lies like lead upon me,
   And yet I would not sleep. Merciful powers,
   Restrain in me the cursed thoughts that nature
   Gives way to in repose!
            Enter Macbeth, *and a* Servant *with a torch*
                           Give me my sword.
   Who's there?

Macbeth. A friend.

Banquo. What, sir, not yet at rest? The king's a-bed:
   He hath been in unusual pleasure, and

Sent forth great largess to your offices:
This diamond he greets your wife withal,
By the name of most kind hostess; and shut up
In measureless content.

Macbeth.   Being unprepared,
Our will became the servant to defect,
Which else should free have wrought.

Banquo.   All's well.
I dreamt last night of the three weïrd sisters:
To you they have show'd some truth.

Macbeth.   I think not of them:
Yet when we can entreat an hour to serve,
We would spend it in some words upon that business,
If you would grant the time.

Banquo.   At your kind'st leisure.

Macbeth. If you shall cleave to my consent, when 'tis,
It shall make honour for you.

Banquo.   So I lose none
In seeking to augment it, but still keep
My bosom franchised and allegiance clear,
I shall be counsell'd.

Macbeth.   Good repose the while!

Banquo. Thanks, sir: the like to you!

                              Exeunt Banquo *and* Fleance.

Macbeth. Go bid thy mistress, when my drink is ready,
She strike upon the bell. Get thee to bed.

                              Exit Servant.

Is this a dagger which I see before me,
The handle toward my hand? Come, let me clutch thee.
I have thee not, and yet I see thee still.
Art thou not, fatal vision, sensible

To feeling as to sight? or art thou but
A dagger of the mind, a false creation,
Proceeding from the heat-oppressed brain?
I see thee yet, in form as palpable
As this which now I draw.
Thou marshall'st me the way that I was going;
And such an instrument I was to use.
Mine eyes are made the fools o' the other senses,
Or else worth all the rest: I see thee still;
And on thy blade and dudgeon gouts of blood,
Which was not so before. There's no such thing:
It is the bloody business which informs
Thus to mine eyes. Now o'er the one half-world
Nature seems dead, and wicked dreams abuse
The curtain'd sleep; witchcraft celebrates
Pale Hecate's offerings; and wither'd murder,
Alarum'd by his sentinel, the wolf,
Whose howl's his watch, thus with his stealthy pace,
With Tarquin's ravishing strides, towards his design
Moves like a ghost. Thou sure and firm-set earth,
Hear not my steps, which way they walk, for fear
Thy very stones prate of my whereabout,
And take the present horror from the time,
Which now suits with it. Whiles I threat, he lives:
Words to the heat of deeds too cold breath gives.

A bell rings.

I go, and it is done: the bell invites me.
Hear it not, Duncan, for it is a knell
That summons thee to heaven, or to hell.

Exit.

scene 2.   [*The same*]

Enter Lady Macbeth

Lady Macbeth. That which hath made them drunk hath made
    me bold;
    What hath quench'd them hath given me fire. Hark! Peace!
    It was the owl that shriek'd, the fatal bellman,
    Which gives the stern'st good-night. He is about it:
    The doors are open, and the surfeited grooms
    Do mock their charge with snores: I have drugg'd their possets,
    That death and nature do contend about them,
    Whether they live or die.

Macbeth.   [*Within*] Who's there? what, ho!

Lady Macbeth. Alack, I am afraid they have awaked
    And 'tis not done: the attempt and not the deed
    Confounds us. Hark! I laid their daggers ready;
    He could not miss 'em. Had he not resembled
    My father as he slept, I had done 't.

                    Enter Macbeth

                         My husband!

Macbeth. I have done the deed. Didst thou not hear a noise?

Lady Macbeth. I heard the owl scream and the crickets cry.
    Did not you speak?

Macbeth.   When?

Lady Macbeth.   Now.

Macbeth.   As I descended?

Lady Macbeth. Ay.

Macbeth. Hark!
    Who lies i' the second chamber?

Lady Macbeth.   Donalbain.

Macbeth. This is a sorry sight.

Looking on his hands.

Lady Macbeth. A foolish thought, to say a sorry sight.

Macbeth. There's one did laugh in 's sleep, and one cried 'Murder!'
That they did wake each other: I stood and heard them:
But they did say their prayers, and address'd them
Again to sleep.

Lady Macbeth.   There are two lodged together.

Macbeth. One cried 'God bless us!' and 'Amen' the other,
As they had seen me with these hangman's hands:
Listening their fear, I could not say 'Amen,'
When they did say 'God bless us!'

Lady Macbeth. Consider it not so deeply.

Macbeth. But wherefore could not I pronounce 'Amen'?
I had most need of blessing, and 'Amen'
Stuck in my throat.

Lady Macbeth.   These deeds must not be thought
After these ways; so, it will make us mad.

Macbeth. Methought I heard a voice cry 'Sleep no more!
Macbeth does murder sleep'—the innocent sleep,
Sleep that knits up the ravell'd sleave of care,
The death of each day's life, sore labour's bath,
Balm of hurt minds, great nature's second course,
Chief nourisher in life's feast,—

Lady Macbeth.   What do you mean?

Macbeth. Still it cried 'Sleep no more!' to all the house:
'Glamis hath murder'd sleep, and therefore Cawdor
Shall sleep no more: Macbeth shall sleep no more.'

Lady Macbeth. Who was it that thus cried? Why, worthy thane,

You do unbend your noble strength, to think
So brainsickly of things. Go get some water,
And wash this filthy witness from your hand.
Why did you bring these daggers from the place?
They must lie there: go carry them, and smear
The sleepy grooms with blood.

Macbeth.   I'll go no more:
I am afraid to think what I have done;
Look on 't again I dare not.

Lady Macbeth.   Infirm of purpose!
Give me the daggers: the sleeping and the dead
Are but as pictures: 'tis the eye of childhood
That fears a painted devil. If he do bleed,
I'll gild the faces of the grooms withal,
For it must seem their guilt.

                              Exit. Knocking within.

Macbeth.   Whence is that knocking?
How is 't with me, when every noise appals me?
What hands are here? ha! they pluck out mine eyes!
Will all great Neptune's ocean wash this blood
Clean from my hand? No; this my hand will rather
The multitudinous seas incarnadine,
Making the green one red.

                    Re-enter Lady Macbeth

Lady Macbeth. My hands are of your colour, but I shame
To wear a heart so white. [*Knocking within*] I hear a knocking
At the south entry: retire we to our chamber:
A little water clears us of this deed:
How easy is it then! Your constancy
Hath left you unattended. [*Knocking within*] Hark! more
    knocking:
Get on your nightgown, lest occasion call us

And show us to be watchers: be not lost
So poorly in your thoughts.

Macbeth. To know my deed, 'twere best not know myself.

Knocking within.

Wake Duncan with thy knocking! I would thou couldst!

Exeunt.

scene 3. [*The same*]

Enter a Porter. *Knocking within*

Porter. Here's a knocking indeed! If a man were porter of Hell
Gate, he should have old turning the key. [*Knocking within*]
Knock, knock, knock! Who's there, i' the name of
Beelzebub? Here's a farmer, that hanged himself on th'
expectation of plenty: come in time; have napkins enow
about you; here you'll sweat for 't. [*Knocking within*] Knock,
knock! Who's there, in th' other devil's name? Faith, here's an
equivocator, that could swear in both the scales against either
scale; who committed treason enough for God's sake, yet
could not equivocate to heaven: O, come in, equivocator.
[*Knocking within*] Knock, knock, knock! Who's there? Faith,
here's an English tailor come hither, for stealing out of a
French hose: come in, tailor; here you may roast your goose.
[*Knocking within*] Knock, knock; never at quiet! What are
you? But this place is too cold for hell. I'll devil-porter it no
further: I had thought to have let in some of all professions,
that go the primrose way to the everlasting bonfire. [*Knocking
within*] Anon, anon! I pray you, remember the Porter.

Opens the gate.

Enter Macduff *and* Lennox

Macduff. Was it so late, friend, ere you went to bed,
That you do lie so late?

Porter. Faith, sir, we were carousing till the second cock: and
drink, sir, is a great provoker of three things.

Macduff. What three things does drink especially provoke?

Porter. Marry, sir, nose-painting, sleep, and urine. Lechery, sir, it
provokes and unprovokes; it provokes the desire, but it takes
away the performance: therefore much drink may be said to
be an equivocator with lechery: it makes him and it mars
him; it sets him on and it takes him off; it persuades him and
disheartens him; makes him stand to and not stand to;
in conclusion, equivocates him in a sleep, and giving him the
lie, leaves him.

Macduff. I believe drink gave thee the lie last night.

Porter. That it did, sir, i' the very throat on me: but I requited
him for his lie, and, I think, being too strong for him, though
he took up my legs sometime, yet I made a shift to cast him.

Macduff. Is thy master stirring?

Enter Macbeth

Our knocking has awaked him; here he comes.

Lennox. Good morrow, noble sir.

Macbeth.   Good morrow, both.

Macduff. Is the king stirring, worthy thane?

Macbeth.   Not yet.

Macduff. He did command me to call timely on him:
I have almost slipp'd the hour.

Macbeth.   I'll bring you to him.

Macduff. I know this is a joyful trouble to you;
But yet 'tis one.

Macbeth. The labour we delight in physics pain.
This is the door.

Macduff.   I'll make so bold to call,
  For 'tis my limited service.

                                        Exit.

Lennox. Goes the king hence to-day?

Macbeth.   He does: he did appoint so.

Lennox. The night has been unruly: where we lay,
  Our chimneys were blown down, and, as they say,
  Lamentings heard i' the air, strange screams of death,
  And prophesying with accents terrible
  Of dire combustion and confused events
  New hatch'd to the woeful time: the obscure bird
  Clamour'd the livelong night: some say, the earth
  Was feverous and did shake.

Macbeth.   'Twas a rough night.

Lennox. My young remembrance cannot parallel
  A fellow to it.

                Re-enter Macduff

Macduff. O horror, horror, horror! Tongue nor heart
  Cannot conceive nor name thee.

Macbeth and Lennox.   What's the matter?

Macduff. Confusion now hath made his masterpiece.
  Most sacrilegious murder hath broke ope
  The Lord's anointed temple, and stole thence
  The life o' the building.

Macbeth.   What is 't you say? the life?

Lennox. Mean you his majesty?

Macduff. Approach the chamber, and destroy your sight
  With a new Gorgon: do not bid me speak;
  See, and then speak yourselves.

                        Exeunt Macbeth *and* Lennox.
                        Awake, awake!

Ring the alarum-bell. Murder and treason!
Banquo and Donalbain! Malcolm! awake!
Shake off this downy sleep, death's counterfeit,
And look on death itself! up, up, and see
The great doom's image! Malcolm! Banquo!
As from your graves rise up, and walk like sprites,
To countenance this horror.

Bell rings.

Enter Lady Macbeth

Lady Macbeth.   What's the business,
That such a hideous trumpet calls to parley
The sleepers of the house? speak, speak!

Macduff.   O gentle lady,
'Tis not for you to hear what I can speak:
The repetition, in a woman's ear,
Would murder as it fell.

Enter Banquo
O Banquo, Banquo!
Our royal master's murder'd.

Lady Macbeth.   Woe, alas!
What, in our house?

Banquo.   Too cruel anywhere.
Dear Duff, I prithee, contradict thyself,
And say it is not so.

Re-enter Macbeth *and* Lennox, *with* Ross

Macbeth. Had I but died an hour before this chance,
I had lived a blessed time; for from this instant
There's nothing serious in mortality:
All is but toys: renown and grace is dead;
The wine of life is drawn, and the mere lees
Is left this vault to brag of.

Enter Malcolm *and* Donalbain

Donalbain. What is amiss?

Macbeth.   You are, and do not know 't:
   The spring, the head, the fountain of your blood
   Is stopp'd; the very source of it is stopp'd.

Macduff. Your royal father's murder'd.

Malcolm.   O! By whom?

Lennox. Those of his chamber, as it seem'd, had done 't:
   Their hands and faces were all badged with blood;
   So were their daggers, which unwiped we found
   Upon their pillows: They stared, and were distracted;
   No man's life
   Was to be trusted with them.

Macbeth. O, yet I do repent me of my fury;
   That I did kill them.

Malcolm.   Wherefore did you so?

Macbeth. Who can be wise, amazed, temperate and furious,
   Loyal and neutral, in a moment? No man:
   The expedition of my violent love
   Outrun the pauser reason. Here lay Duncan,
   His silver skin laced with his golden blood,
   And his gash'd stabs look'd like a breach in nature
   For ruin's wasteful entrance: there, the murderers,
   Steep'd in the colours of their trade, their daggers
   Unmannerly breech'd with gore: who could refrain,
   That had a heart to love, and in that heart
   Courage to make 's love known?

Lady Macbeth.   Help me hence, ho!

Macduff. Look to the lady.

Malcolm. [*Aside to Donalbain*] Why do we hold our tongues,
   That most may claim this argument for ours?

Donalbain. [*Aside to Malcolm*] What should be spoken here,
where our fate, hid in an auger-hole,
May rush, and seize us? Let's away;
Our tears are not yet brew'd.

Malcolm. [*Aside to Donalbain*] Nor our strong sorrow
Upon the foot of motion.

Banquo.   Look to the lady:

                                        Lady Macbeth is carried out.

And when we have our naked frailties hid,
That suffer in exposure, let us meet,
And question this most bloody piece of work,
To know it further. Fears and scruples shake us:
In the great hand of God I stand, and thence
Against the undivulged pretence I fight
Of treasonous malice.

Macduff.   And so do I.

All.   So all.

Macbeth. Let's briefly put on manly readiness,
And meet i' the hall together.

All.   Well contented.

                      Exeunt all but Malcolm *and* Donalbain.

Malcolm. What will you do? Let's not consort with them:
To show an unfelt sorrow is an office
Which the false man does easy. I'll to England.

Donalbain. To Ireland, I; our separated fortune
Shall keep us both the safer; where we are
There's daggers in men's smiles: the near in blood,
The nearer bloody.

Malcolm.   This murderous shaft that's shot
Hath not yet lighted, and our safest way
Is to avoid the aim. Therefore to horse;
And let us not be dainty of leave-taking,

But shift away: there's warrant in that theft
Which steals itself when there's no mercy left.

Exeunt.

scene 4.   [*Outside* Macbeth's *castle*]

Enter Ross *with an* Old Man

Old Man. Threescore and ten I can remember well:
Within the volume of which time I have seen
Hours dreadful and things strange, but this sore night
Hath trifled former knowings.

Ross.   Ah, good father,
Thou seest the heavens, as troubled with man's act,
Threaten his bloody stage: by the clock 'tis day,
And yet dark night strangles the travelling lamp:
Is 't night's predominance, or the day's shame,
That darkness does the face of earth entomb,
When living light should kiss it?

Old Man.   'Tis unnatural,
Even like the deed that's done. On Tuesday last
A falcon towering in her pride of place
Was by a mousing owl hawk'd at and kill'd.

Ross. And Duncan's horses—a thing most strange and certain—
Beauteous and swift, the minions of their race,
Turn'd wild in nature, broke their stalls, flung out,
Contending 'gainst obedience, as they would make
War with mankind.

Old Man.   'Tis said they eat each other.

Ross. They did so, to th' amazement of mine eyes,
That look'd upon 't.

Enter Macduff

                    Here comes the good Macduff
  How goes the world, sir, now?

Macduff.   Why, see you not?

Ross. Is 't known who did this more than bloody deed?

Macduff. Those that Macbeth hath slain.

Ross.   Alas, the day!
  What good could they pretend?

Macduff.   They were suborn'd:
  Malcolm and Donalbain, the king's two sons,
  Are stol'n away and fled, which puts upon them
  Suspicion of the deed.

Ross.   'Gainst nature still:
  Thriftless Ambition, that wilt ravin up
  Thine own life's means! Then 'tis most like
  The sovereignty will fall upon Macbeth.

Macduff. He is already named, and gone to Scone
  To be invested.

Ross.   Where is Duncan's body?

Macduff. Carried to Colme-kill,
  The sacred storehouse of his predecessors
  And guardian of their bones.

Ross.   Will you to Scone?

Macduff. No, cousin, I'll to Fife.

Ross.   Well, I will thither.

Macduff. Well, may you see things well done there: adieu!
  Lest our old robes sit easier than our new!

Ross. Farewell, father.

Old Man. God's benison go with you, and with those
  That would make good of bad, and friends of foes!

                                   Exeunt.

act 3

Enter Banquo

Banquo. Thou hast it now: king, Cawdor, Glamis, all,
  As the weïrd women promised, and I fear
  Thou play'dst most foully for 't: yet it was said
  It should not stand in thy posterity,
  But that myself should be the root and father
  Of many kings. If there come truth from them—
  As upon thee, Macbeth, their speeches shine—
  Why, by the verities on thee made good,
  May they not be my oracles as well
  And set me up in hope? But hush, no more.
      Sennet sounded. Enter Macbeth, *as king;* Lady
          Macbeth, *as queen;* Lennox, Ross, Lords,
              Ladies, *and* Attendants

Macbeth. Here's our chief guest.

Lady Macbeth.   If he had been forgotten,
  It had been as a gap in our great feast,
  And all-thing unbecoming.

Macbeth. To-night we hold a solemn supper, sir,
  And I'll request your presence.

Banquo.   Let your highness
  Command upon me, to the which my duties
  Are with a most indissoluble tie
  For ever knit.

Macbeth. Ride you this afternoon?

Banquo.   Ay, my good lord.

Macbeth. We should have else desired your good advice,
  Which still hath been both grave and prosperous,
  In this day's council; but we'll take to-morrow.
  Is 't far you ride?

Banquo. As far, my lord, as will fill up the time
  'Twixt this and supper: go not my horse the better,
  I must become a borrower of the night
  For a dark hour or twain.

Macbeth.   Fail not our feast.

Banquo. My lord, I will not.

Macbeth. We hear our bloody cousins are bestow'd
  In England and in Ireland, not confessing
  Their cruel parricide, filling their hearers
  With strange invention: but of that to-morrow,
  When therewithal we shall have cause of state
  Craving us jointly. Hie you to horse: adieu,
  Till you return at night. Goes Fleance with you?

Banquo. Ay, my good lord: our time does call upon 's.

Macbeth. I wish your horses swift and sure of foot,
  And so I do commend you to their backs.
  Farewell.

                                        Exit Banquo.

Let every man be master of his time
Till seven at night; to make society
The sweeter welcome, we will keep ourself
Till supper-time alone: while then, God be with you!

               Exeunt all but Macbeth *and an* Attendant.

Sirrah, a word with you: attend those men
Our pleasure?

Attendant. They are, my lord, without the palace-gate.

Macbeth. Bring them before us.

                                 Exit Attendant.

                  To be thus is nothing, But to be safely thus:
Our fears in Banquo
Stick deep; and in his royalty of nature
Reigns that which would be fear'd: 'tis much he dares,
And, to that dauntless temper of his mind,
He hath a wisdom that doth guide his valour
To act in safety. There is none but he
Whose being I do fear: and under him
My Genius is rebuked, as it is said,
Mark Antony's was by Cæsar. He chid the sisters,
When first they put the name of king upon me,
And bade them speak to him; then prophet-like
They hail'd him father to a line of kings:
Upon my head they placed a fruitless crown
And put a barren sceptre in my gripe,
Thence to be wrench'd with an unlineal hand,
No son of mine succeeding. If 't be so,
For Banquo's issue have I filed my mind;
For them the gracious Duncan have I murder'd;
Put rancours in the vessel of my peace
Only for them, and mine eternal jewel
Given to the common enemy of man,

To make them kings, the seed of Banquo kings!
Rather than so, come, fate, into the list,
And champion me to th' utterance! Who's there?

    Re-enter Attendant, *with* Two Murderers

Now go to the door, and stay there till we call.

           Exit Attendant.

Was it not yesterday we spoke together?

First Murderer. It was, so please your highness.

Macbeth.   Well then, now
Have you consider'd of my speeches? Know
That it was he in the times past which held you
So under fortune, which you thought had been
Our innocent self? This I made good to you
In our last conference; pass'd in probation with you,
How you were borne in hand, how cross'd, the instruments,
Who wrought with them, and all things else that might
To half a soul and to a notion crazed
Say 'Thus did Banquo.'

First Murderer.   You made it known to us.

Macbeth. I did so; and went further, which is now
Our point of second meeting. Do you find
Your patience so predominant in your nature,
That you can let this go? Are you so gospell'd,
To pray for this good man and for his issue,
Whose heavy hand hath bow'd you to the grave
And beggar'd yours for ever?

First Murderer.   We are men, my liege.

Macbeth. Ay, in the catalogue ye go for men;
As hounds and greyhounds, mongrels, spaniels, curs,
Shoughs, water-rugs and demi-wolves, are clept
All by the name of dogs: the valued file
Distinguishes the swift, the slow, the subtle,

The housekeeper, the hunter, every one
According to the gift which bounteous Nature
Hath in him closed, whereby he does receive
Particular addition, from the bill
That writes them all alike: and so of men.
Now if you have a station in the file,
Not i' the worst rank of manhood, say it,
And I will put that business in your bosoms
Whose execution takes your enemy off,
Grapples you to the heart and love of us,
Who wear our health but sickly in his life,
Which in his death were perfect.

Second Murderer.   I am one, my liege,
Whom the vile blows and buffets of the world
Have so incensed that I am reckless what
I do to spite the world.

First Murderer.   And I another
So weary with disasters, tugg'd with fortune,
That I would set my life on any chance,
To mend it or be rid on 't.

Macbeth.   Both of you
Know Banquo was your enemy.

Both Murderers.   True, my lord.

Macbeth. So is he mine, and in such bloody distance
That every minute of his being thrusts
Against my near'st of life: and though I could
With barefaced power sweep him from my sight
And bid my will avouch it, yet I must not,
For certain friends that are both his and mine,
Whose loves I may not drop, but wail his fall
Who I myself struck down: and thence it is
That I to your assistance do make love,

Masking the business from the common eye
For sundry weighty reasons.

Second Murderer.   We shall, my lord,
Perform what you command us.

First Murderer.   Though our lives—

Macbeth. Your spirits shine through you. Within this hour at
 most
I will advise you where to plant yourselves,
Acquaint you with the perfect spy o' the time,
The moment on 't; for 't must be done to-night,
And something from the palace; always thought
That I require a clearness: and with him—
To leave no rubs nor botches in the work—
Fleance his son, that keeps him company,
Whose absence is no less material to me
Than is his father's, must embrace the fate
Of that dark hour. Resolve yourselves apart:
I'll come to you anon.

Both Murderers.   We are resolved, my lord.

Macbeth. I'll call upon you straight: abide within.

          Exeunt Murderers.

It is concluded: Banquo, thy soul's flight,
If it find heaven, must find it out to-night.

            Exit.

scene 2. [*The palace*]

Enter Lady Macbeth *and a* Servant

Lady Macbeth. Is Banquo gone from court?

Servant. Ay, madam, but returns again to-night.

Lady Macbeth. Say to the king, I would attend his leisure
  For a few words.

Servant.   Madam, I will.

                                                Exit.

Lady Macbeth.   Nought's had, all's spent,
  Where our desire is got without content:
  'Tis safer to be that which we destroy
  Than by destruction dwell in doubtful joy.
              Enter Macbeth
  How now, my lord? why do you keep alone,
  Of sorriest fancies your companions making;
  Using those thoughts which should indeed have died
  With them they think on? Things without all remedy
  Should be without regard: What's done is done.

Macbeth. We have scorch'd the snake, not kill'd it:
  She'll close and be herself, whilst our poor malice
  Remains in danger of her former tooth.
  But let the frame of things disjoint, both the worlds suffer,
  Ere we will eat our meal in fear, and sleep
  In the affliction of these terrible dreams
  That shake us nightly: better be with the dead,
  Whom we, to gain our peace, have sent to peace,
  Than on the torture of the mind to lie
  In restless ecstasy. Duncan is in his grave;
  After life's fitful fever he sleeps well;
  Treason has done his worst: nor steel, nor poison,
  Malice domestic, foreign levy, nothing
  Can touch him further.

Lady Macbeth.   Come on;
  Gentle my lord, sleek o'er your rugged looks;
  Be bright and jovial among your guests to-night.

Macbeth. So shall I, love; and so, I pray, be you:
  Let your remembrance apply to Banquo;
  Present him eminence, both with eye and tongue:
  Unsafe the while, that we
  Must lave our honours in these flattering streams,
  And make our faces visards to our hearts,
  Disguising what they are.

Lady Macbeth.   You must leave this.

Macbeth. O, full of scorpions is my mind, dear wife!
  Thou know'st that Banquo, and his Fleance, lives.

Lady Macbeth. But in them nature's copy's not eterne.

Macbeth. There's comfort yet; they are assailable;
  Then be thou jocund: ere the bat hath flown
  His cloister'd flight; ere to black Hecate's summons
  The shard-borne beetle with his drowsy hums
  Hath rung night's yawning peal, there shall be done
  A deed of dreadful note.

Lady Macbeth.   What's to be done?

Macbeth. Be innocent of the knowledge, dearest chuck,
  Till thou applaud the deed. Come, seeling Night,
  Scarf up the tender eye of pitiful day,
  And with thy bloody and invisible hand
  Cancel and tear to pieces that great bond
  Which keeps me pale! Light thickens, and the crow
  Makes wing to the rooky wood:
  Good things of day begin to droop and drowse,
  Whiles night's black agents to their preys do rouse.
  Thou marvell'st at my words: but hold thee still;
  Things bad begun make strong themselves by ill:
  So, prithee, go with me.

                                        Exeunt.

scene 3.   [*A park near the palace*]

Enter Three Murderers

First Murderer. But who did bid thee join with us?

Third Murderer.   Macbeth.

Second Murderer. He needs not our mistrust; since he delivers
    Our offices, and what we have to do,
    To the direction just.

First Murderer.   Then stand with us.
    The west yet glimmers with some streaks of day:
    Now spurs the lated traveller apace
    To gain the timely inn, and near approaches
    The subject of our watch.

Third Murderer.   Hark! I hear horses.

Banquo. [Within] Give us a light there, ho!

Second Murderer.   Then 'tis he: the rest
    That are within the note of expectation
    Already are i' the court.

First Murderer.   His horses go about.

Third Murderer. Almost a mile: but he does usually—
    So all men do—from hence to the palace gate
    Make it their walk.

Second Murderer.   A light, a light!
                Enter Banquo, *and* Fleance *with a torch*

Third Murderer.   'Tis he.

First Murderer. Stand to 't.

Banquo. It will be rain to-night.

First Murderer.   Let it come down.

> *They set upon* Banquo.

Banquo. O, treachery! Fly, good Fleance, fly, fly, fly!
Thou mayst revenge. O slave!

> *Dies.* Fleance *escapes.*

Third Murderer. Who did strike out the light?

First Murderer.   Was't not the way?

Third Murderer. There's but one down; the son is fled.

Second Murderer.   We have lost
Best half of our affair.

First Murderer. Well, let's away and say how much is done.

> *Exeunt.*

scene 4.   [*Hall in the palace*]

A banquet prepared. Enter Macbeth, Lady Macbeth,
Ross, Lennox, Lords, *and* Attendants

Macbeth. You know your own degrees; sit down: at first
And last the hearty welcome.

Lords.   Thanks to your majesty.

Macbeth. Ourself will mingle with society
And play the humble host.
Our hostess keeps her state, but in best time
We will require her welcome.

Lady Macbeth. Pronounce it for me, sir, to all our friends,
For my heart speaks they are welcome.

> *Enter* First Murderer *to the door*

Macbeth. See, they encounter thee with their hearts' thanks.
Both sides are even: here I'll sit i' the midst:

Be large in mirth; anon we'll drink a measure
The table round. [*Approaching the door*] There's blood upon
    thy face.

Murderer. 'Tis Banquo's then.

Macbeth. 'Tis better thee without than he within.
    Is he dispatch'd?

Murderer. My lord, his throat is cut; that I did for him.

Macbeth. Thou art the best o' the cut-throats: yet he's good
    That did the like for Fleance: if thou didst it,
    Thou art the nonpareil.

Murderer.   Most royal sir,
    Fleance is 'scaped.

Macbeth. [*Aside*] Then comes my fit again: I had else been
    perfect,
    Whole as the marble, founded as the rock,
    As broad and general as the casing air:
    But now I am cabin'd, cribb'd confined, bound in
    To saucy doubts and fears.—But Banquo's safe?

Murderer. Ay, my good lord: safe in a ditch he bides,
    With twenty trenched gashes on his head;
    The least a death to nature.

Macbeth.   Thanks for that.
    [*Aside*] There the grown serpent lies; the worm that's fled
    Hath nature that in time will venom breed,
    No teeth for the present. Get thee gone: to-morrow
    We'll hear ourselves again.

                                        Exit Murderer.

Lady Macbeth. My royal lord,
    You do not give the cheer: the feast is sold
    That is not often vouch'd, while 'tis a-making,
    'Tis given with welcome: to feed were best at home;

From thence the sauce to meat is ceremony;
Meeting were bare without it.

Macbeth.   Sweet remembrancer!
Now good digestion wait on appetite,
And health on both!

Lennox.   May't please your highness sit.

Macbeth. Here had we now our country's honour roof'd,
Were the graced person of our Banquo present;
Who may I rather challenge for unkindness
Than pity for mischance!
    The Ghost of Banquo *enters, and sits in* Macbeth's *place*

Ross.   His absence, sir,
Lays blame upon his promise. Please 't your highness
To grace us with your royal company?

Macbeth. The table's full.

Lennox.   Here is a place reserved, sir.

Macbeth. Where?

Lennox. Here, my good lord. What is 't that moves your highness?

Macbeth. Which of you have done this?

Lords.   What, my good lord?

Macbeth. Thou canst not say I did it: never shake
Thy gory locks at me.

Ross. Gentlemen, rise; his highness is not well.

Lady Macbeth. Sit, worthy friends: my lord is often thus,
And hath been from his youth: pray you, keep seat;
The fit is momentary; upon a thought
He will again be well: if much you note him,
You shall offend him and extend his passion:
Feed, and regard him not. Are you a man?

Macbeth. Ay, and a bold one, that dare look on that
    Which might appal the devil.

Lady Macbeth.   O proper stuff!
    This is the very painting of your fear:
    This is the air-drawn dagger which, you said,
    Led you to Duncan. O, these flaws and starts,
    Impostors to true fear, would well become
    A woman's story at a winter's fire,
    Authorized by her grandam. Shame itself!
    Why do you make such faces? When all's done,
    You look but on a stool.

Macbeth. Prithee, see there!
    Behold! look! lo! how say you?
    Why, what care I? If thou canst nod, speak too.
    If charnel-houses and our graves must send
    Those that we bury back, our monuments
    Shall be the maws of kites.

                                        Exit Ghost.

Lady Macbeth.   What, quite unmann'd in folly?

Macbeth. If I stand here, I saw him.

Lady Macbeth.   Fie, for shame!

Macbeth. Blood hath been shed ere now, i' the olden time,
    Ere humane statute purged the gentle weal;
    Ay, and since too, murders have been perform'd
    Too terrible for the ear: the time has been,
    That, when the brains were out, the man would die,
    And there an end; but now they rise again,
    With twenty mortal murders on their crowns,
    And push us from our stools: this is more strange
    Than such a murder is.

Lady Macbeth.   My worthy lord,
   Your noble friends do lack you.

Macbeth.   I do forget.
   Do not muse at me, my most worthy friends;
   I have a strange infirmity, which is nothing
   To those that know me. Come, love and health to all;
   Then I'll sit down. Give me some wine, fill full.
   I drink to the general joy o' the whole table,
   And to our dear friend Banquo, whom we miss;
   Would he were here! to all and him we thirst,
   And all to all.

Lords.   Our duties, and the pledge.

                      Re-enter Ghost

Macbeth. Avaunt! and quit my sight! let the earth hide thee!
   Thy bones are marrowless, thy blood is cold;
   Thou hast no speculation in those eyes
   Which thou dost glare with.

Lady Macbeth.   Think of this, good peers,
   But as a thing of custom: 'tis no other;
   Only it spoils the pleasure of the time.

Macbeth. What man dare, I dare:
   Approach thou like the rugged Russian bear,
   The arm'd rhinoceros, or the Hyrcan tiger;
   Take any shape but that, and my firm nerves
   Shall never tremble: or be alive again,
   And dare me to the desert with thy sword;
   If trembling I inhabit then, protest me
   The baby of a girl. Hence, horrible shadow!
   Unreal mockery, hence!

                                          Exit Ghost.

                    Why, so: being gone,
   I am a man again. Pray you, sit still.

Lady Macbeth. You have displaced the mirth, broke the good
    meeting,
    With most admired disorder.

Macbeth.   Can such things be,
    And overcome us like a summer's cloud,
    Without our special wonder? You make me strange
    Even to the disposition that I owe,
    When now I think you can behold such sights,
    And keep the natural ruby of your cheeks,
    When mine is blanch'd with fear.

Ross.   What sights, my lord?

Lady Macbeth. I pray you, speak not; he grows worse and worse;
    Question enrages him: at once, good night:
    Stand not upon the order of your going,
    But go at once.

Lennox.   Good night; and better health
    Attend his majesty!

Lady Macbeth. A kind good night to all!
                    Exeunt all but Macbeth *and* Lady Macbeth.

Macbeth. It will have blood, they say: blood will have blood:
    Stones have been known to move and trees to speak;
    Augures and understood relations have
    By maggot-pies and choughs and rooks brought forth
    The secret'st man of blood. What is the night?

Lady Macbeth. Almost at odds with morning, which is which.

Macbeth. How say'st thou, that Macduff denies his person
    At our great bidding?

Lady Macbeth.   Did you send to him, sir?

Macbeth. I hear it by the way, but I will send:
    There's not a one of them but in his house

I keep a servant fee'd. I will to-morrow,
And betimes I will, to the weïrd sisters:
More shall they speak, for now I am bent to know,
By the worst means, the worst. For mine own good
All causes shall give way: I am in blood
Stepp'd in so far that, should I wade no more,
Returning were as tedious as go o'er:
Strange things I have in head that will to hand,
Which must be acted ere they may be scann'd.

Lady Macbeth. You lack the season of all natures, sleep.

Macbeth. Come, we'll to sleep. My strange and self-abuse
Is the initiate fear that wants hard use:
We are yet but young in deed.

Exeunt.

scene 5. [*A heath*]

Thunder. Enter the Three Witches, *meeting* Hecate

First Witch. Why, how now, Hecate! you look angerly.

Hecate. Have I not reason, beldams as you are,
Saucy and over-bold? How did you dare
To trade and traffic with Macbeth
In riddles and affairs of death;
And I, the mistress of your charms,
The close contriver of all harms,
Was never call'd to bear my part,
Or show the glory of our art?
And, which is worse, all you have done
Hath been but for a wayward son,
Spiteful and wrathful; who, as others do,
Loves for his own ends, not for you.

But make amends now: get you gone,
And at the pit of Acheron
Meet me i' the morning: thither he
Will come to know his destiny:
Your vessels and your spells provide,
Your charms and every thing beside.
I am for th' air; this night I'll spend
Unto a dismal and a fatal end:
Great business must be wrought ere noon:
Upon the corner of the moon
There hangs a vaporous drop profound;
I'll catch it ere it come to ground:
And that distill'd by magic sleights
Shall raise such artificial sprites
As by the strength of their illusion
Shall draw him on to his confusion:
He shall spurn fate, scorn death, and bear
His hopes 'bove wisdom, grace and fear:
And you all know security
Is mortals' chiefest enemy.

> *Music and a song within:*
> 'Come away, come away,' & *c.*

Hark! I am call'd; my little spirit, see,
Sits in a foggy cloud, and stays for me.

> *Exit.*

First Witch. Come, let's make haste; she'll soon be back again.

> *Exeunt.*

scene 6. *[Forres. The palace]*

Enter Lennox *and another* Lord

Lennox. My former speeches have but hit your thoughts,
    Which can interpret farther: only I say
    Things have been strangely borne. The gracious
        Duncan
    Was pitied of Macbeth: marry, he was dead:
    And the right-valiant Banquo walk'd too late;
    Whom, you may say, if 't please you, Fleance kill'd,
    For Fleance fled: men must not walk too late.
    Who cannot want the thought, how monstrous
    It was for Malcolm and for Donalbain
    To kill their gracious father? damned fact!
    How it did grieve Macbeth! did he not straight,
    In pious rage, the two delinquents tear,
    That were the slaves of drink and thralls of sleep?
    Was not that nobly done? Ay, and wisely too;
    For 'twould have anger'd any heart alive
    To hear the men deny 't. So that, I say,
    He has borne all things well: and I do think
    That, had he Duncan's sons under his key—
    As, an 't please heaven, he shall not—they should find
    What 'twere to kill a father; so should Fleance.
    But, peace! for from broad words, and 'cause he fail'd
    His presence at the tyrant's feast, I hear,
    Macduff lives in disgrace: sir, can you tell
    Where he bestows himself?

Lord.   The son of Duncan,
    From whom this tyrant holds the due of birth,

Lives in the English court, and is received
Of the most pious Edward with such grace
That the malevolence of fortune nothing
Takes from his high respect. Thither Macduff
Is gone to pray the holy king, upon his aid
To wake Northumberland and warlike Siward:
That by the help of these, with Him above
To ratify the work, we may again
Give to our tables meat, sleep to our nights,
Free from our feasts and banquets bloody knives,
Do faithful homage and receive free honours:
All which we pine for now: and this report
Hath so exasperate the king that he
Prepares for some attempt of war.

Lennox.   Sent he to Macduff?

Lord. He did: and with an absolute 'sir, not I,'
   The cloudy messenger turns me his back,
   And hums, as who should say 'You'll rue the time
   That clogs me with this answer.'

Lennox.   And that well might
   Advise him to a caution, to hold what distance
   His wisdom cart provide. Some holy angel
   Fly to the court of England and unfold
   His message ere he come, that a swift blessing
   May soon return to this our suffering country
   Under a hand accursed!

Lord.   I'll send my prayers with him.

                                          Exeunt.

act 4

[*A cavern. In the middle, a boiling cauldron*]

Thunder. Enter the Three Witches

First Witch. Thrice the brinded cat hath mew'd.

Second Witch. Thrice, and once the hedge-pig whined.

Third Witch. Harpier cries 'Tis time, 'tis time.

First Witch. Round about the cauldron go:
   In the poison'd entrails throw.
   Toad, that under cold stone
   Days and nights has thirty one
   Swelter'd venom, sleeping got,
   Boil thou first i' the charmed pot.

All. Double, double toil and trouble;
   Fire burn and cauldron bubble.

Second Witch. Fillet of a feny snake,
   In the cauldron boil and bake;
   Eye of newt and toe of frog,
   Wool of bat and tongue of dog,
   Adder's fork and blind-worm's sting,

Lizard's leg and howlet's wing,
For a charm of powerful trouble,
Like a hell-broth boil and bubble.

All. Double, double toil and trouble;
Fire burn and cauldron bubble.

Third Witch. Scale of dragon, tooth of wolf,
Witches' mummy, maw and gulf
Of the ravin'd salt-sea shark,
Root of hemlock digg'd i' the dark,
Liver of blaspheming Jew,
Gall of goat and slips of yew
Silver'd in the moon's eclipse,
Nose of Turk and Tartar's lips,
Finger of birth-strangled babe
Ditch-deliver'd by a drab,
Make the gruel thick and slab:
Add thereto a tiger's chaudron,
For the ingredients of our cauldron.

All. Double, double toil and trouble;
Fire burn and cauldron bubble.

Second Witch. Cool it with a baboon's blood,
Then the charm is firm and good.

> *Enter* Hecate *to the other* Three Witches

Hecate. O, well done! I commend your pains;
And every one shall share i' the gains:
And now about the cauldron sing,
Like elves and fairies in a ring,
Enchanting all that you put in.

> *Music and song:* 'Black Spirits,' & c.
>
> Hecate *retires.*

Second Witch. By the pricking of my thumbs,
Something wicked this way comes:

    Open, locks,
    Whoever knocks!

Enter Macbeth

Macbeth. How now, you secret, black, and midnight hags!
    What is 't you do?

All.   A deed without a name.

Macbeth. I conjure you, by that which you profess,
    Howe'er you come to know it, answer me:
    Though you untie the winds and let them fight
    Against the churches; though the yesty waves
    Confound and swallow navigation up;
    Though bladed corn be lodged and trees blown down;
    Though castles topple on their warders' heads;
    Though palaces and pyramids do slope
    Their heads to their foundations; though the treasure
    Of nature's germins tumble all together,
    Even till destruction sicken; answer me
    To what I ask you.

First Witch.   Speak.

Second Witch.   Demand.

Third Witch.   We'll answer.

First Witch. Say, if thou'dst rather hear it from our mouths,
    Or from our masters.

Macbeth.   Call 'em, let me see 'em.

First Witch. Pour in sow's blood, that hath eaten
    Her nine farrow; grease that's sweaten
    From the murderer's gibbet, throw
    Into the flame.

All.   Come, high or low;
    Thyself and office deftly show!

Thunder. First Apparition: *an armed Head*

Macbeth. Tell me, thou unknown power,—

First Witch.   He knows thy thought:
  Hear his speech, but say thou nought.

First Apparition. Macbeth! Macbeth! Macbeth! beware Macduff;
  Beware the thane of Fife. Dismiss me: enough.

                                     Descends.

Macbeth. Whate'er thou art, for thy good caution thanks;
  Thou hast harp'd my fear aright: but one word more,—

First Witch. He will not be commanded: here's another,
  More potent than the first.
        Thunder. Second Apparition: *a bloody Child*

Second Apparition. Macbeth! Macbeth! Macbeth!

Macbeth. Had I three ears, I'd hear thee.

Second Apparition. Be bloody, bold, and resolute; laugh to scorn
  The power of man, for none of woman born
  Shall harm Macbeth.

                                       Descends.

Macbeth. Then live, Macduff: what need I fear of thee?
  But yet I'll make assurance double sure,
  And take a bond of fate: thou shalt not live;
  That I may tell pale-hearted fear it lies,
  And sleep in spite of thunder.

Thunder. Third Apparition: *a Child crowned, with a tree in his hand*
                             What is this,
  That rises like the issue of a king,
  And wears upon his baby-brow the round
  And top of sovereignty?

All. Listen, but speak not to 't.

Third Apparition. Be lion-mettled, proud, and take no care
    Who chafes, who frets, or where conspirers are:
    Macbeth shall never vanquish'd be until
    Great Birnam wood to high Dunsinane hill
    Shall come against him.

                        Descends.

Macbeth.   That will never be:
    Who can impress the forest, bid the tree
    Unfix his earth-bound root? Sweet bodements! good!
    Rebellious dead, rise never, till the wood
    Of Birnam rise, and our high-placed Macbeth
    Shall live the lease of nature, pay his breath
    To time and mortal custom. Yet my heart
    Throbs to know one thing: tell me, if you art
    Can tell so much: shall Banquo's issue ever
    Reign in this kingdom?

All. Seek to know no more.

Macbeth. I will be satisfied: deny me this,
    And an eternal curse fall on you! Let me know:
    Why sinks that cauldron? and what noise is this?

                        Hautboys.

First Witch. Show!

Second Witch. Show!

Third Witch. Show!

All. Show his eyes, and grieve his heart;
    Come like shadows, so depart!
       A show of eight Kings, *the last with a glass in his hand;*
               Banquo's Ghost *following*

Macbeth. Thou art too like the spirit of Banquo: down!
    Thy crown does sear mine eye-balls. And thy hair,
    Thou other gold-bound brow, is like the first.

A third is like the former. Filthy hags!
Why do you show me this? A fourth! Start, eyes!
What, will the line stretch out to the crack of doom?
Another yet! A seventh! I'll see no more:
And yet the eighth appears, who bears a glass
Which shows me many more; and some I see
That two-fold balls and treble sceptres carry:
Horrible sight! Now I see 'tis true;
For the blood-bolter'd Banquo smiles upon me,
And points at them for his. What, is this so?

First Witch. Ay, sir, all this is so: but why
Stands Macbeth thus amazedly?
Come, sisters, cheer we up his sprites,
And show the best of our delights:
I'll charm the air to give a sound,
While you perform your antic round,
That this great king may kindly say
Our duties did his welcome pay.

   Music. The Witches *dance, and then vanish, with* Hecate.

Macbeth. Where are they? Gone? Let this pernicious hour
Stand aye accursed in the calendar!
Come in, without there!

    Enter Lennox

Lennox.   What's your grace's will?

Macbeth. Saw you the weïrd sisters?

Lennox.   No, my lord.

Macbeth. Came they not by you?

Lennox.   No indeed, my lord.

Macbeth. Infected be the air whereon they ride,
And damn'd all those that trust them! I did hear
The galloping of horse: who was 't came by?

Lennox. 'Tis two or three, my lord, that bring you word
   Macduff is fled to England.

Macbeth.   Fled to England!

Lennox. Ay, my good lord.

Macbeth. [*Aside*] Time, thou anticipat'st my dread exploits:
   The flighty purpose never is o'ertook
   Unless the deed go with it: from this moment
   The very firstlings of my heart shall be
   The firstlings of my hand. And even now,
   To crown my thoughts with acts, be it thought and done:
   The castle of Macduff I will surprise;
   Seize upon Fife; give to the edge o' the sword
   His wife, his babes, and all unfortunate souls
   That trace him in his line. No boasting like a fool;
   This deed I'll do before this purpose cool:
   But no more sights!—Where are these gentlemen?
   Come, bring me where they are.

                                       Exeunt.

scene 2.   [*Fife*. Macduff's *castle*]

Enter Lady Macduff, *her* Son, *and* Ross

Lady Macduff. What had he done, to make him fly the land?

Ross. You must have patience, madam.

Lady Macduff.   He had none:
   His flight was madness: when our actions do not,
   Our fears do make us traitors.

Ross.   You know not
   Whether it was his wisdom or his fear.

Lady Macduff. Wisdom! to leave his wife, to leave his babes,

His mansion and his titles, in a place
From whence himself does fly? He loves us not;
He wants the natural touch: for the poor wren,
The most diminutive of birds, will fight,
Her young ones in her nest, against the owl.
All is the fear and nothing is the love;
As little is the wisdom, where the flight
So runs against all reason.

Ross.   My dearest coz,
I pray you, school yourself: but, for your husband,
He is noble, wise, judicious, and best knows
The fits o' the season. I dare not speak much further:
But cruel are the times, when we are traitors
And do not know ourselves; when we hold rumour
From what we fear, yet know not what we fear,
But float upon a wild and violent sea
Each way and move. I take my leave of you:
Shall not be long but I'll be here again:
Things at the worst will cease, or else climb upward
To what they were before. My pretty cousin,
Blessing upon you!

Lady Macduff. Father'd he is, and yet he's fatherless.

Ross. I am so much a fool, should I stay longer,
It would be my disgrace and your discomfort:
I take my leave at once.

                                              Exit.

Lady Macduff.   Sirrah, your father's dead:
And what will you do now? How will you live?

Son. As birds do, mother.

Lady Macduff.   What, with worms and flies?

Son. With what I get, I mean; and so do they.

Lady Macduff. Poor bird! thou'dst never fear the net nor lime,
The pitfall nor the gin.

Son. Why should I, mother? Poor birds they are not set for.
My father is not dead, for all your saying.

Lady Macduff. Yes, he is dead: how wilt thou do for a father?

Son. Nay, how will you do for a husband?

Lady Macduff. Why, I can buy me twenty at any market.

Son. Then you'll buy 'em to sell again.

Lady Macduff. Thou speak'st with all thy wit, and yet, i' faith,
With wit enough for thee.

Son. Was my father a traitor, mother?

Lady Macduff. Ay, that he was.

Son. What is a traitor?

Lady Macduff. Why, one that swears and lies.

Son. And be all traitors that do so?

Lady Macduff. Every one that does so is a traitor, and must be
hanged.

Son. And must they all be hanged that swear and lie?

Lady Macduff. Every one.

Son. Who must hang them?

Lady Macduff. Why, the honest men.

Son. Then the liars and swearers are fools; for there are liars and
swearers enow to beat the honest men and hang up them.

Lady Macduff. Now, God help thee, poor monkey! But how wilt
thou do for a father?

Son. If he were dead, you'd weep for him: if you would not,
it were a good sign that I should quickly have a new father.

Lady Macduff. Poor prattler, how thou talk'st!

Enter a Messenger

Messenger. Bless you, fair dame! I am not to you known,
    Though in your state of honour I am perfect.
    I doubt some danger does approach you nearly:
    If you will take a homely man's advice,
    Be not found here; hence, with your little ones.
    To fright you thus, methinks I am too savage;
    To do worse to you were fell cruelty,
    Which is too nigh your person. Heaven preserve you!
    I dare abide no longer.

                                       Exit.

Lady Macduff.   Whither should I fly?
    I have done no harm. But I remember now
    I am in this earthly world, where to do harm
    Is often laudable, to do good sometime
    Accounted dangerous folly: why then, alas,
    Do I put up that womanly defence,
    To say I have done no harm?—What are these faces?
                    Enter Murderers

First Murderer. Where is your husband?

Lady Macduff. I hope, in no place so unsanctified
    Where such as thou mayst find him.

First Murderer.   He's a traitor.

Son. Thou liest, thou shag-ear'd villain!

First Murderer.   What, you egg!
                         Stabbing him.

    Young fry of treachery!

Son.   He has kill'd me, mother:
    Run away, I pray you!

                                Dies.
               Exit Lady Macduff, *crying* 'Murder!'
               Exeunt Murderers, *following her.*

scene 3. [*England. Before the* King's *palace*]

Enter Malcolm *and* Macduff

Malcolm. Let us seek out some desolate shade, and there
  Weep our sad bosoms empty.

Macduff.   Let us rather
  Hold fast the mortal sword, and like good men
  Bestride our down-fall'n birthdom: each new morn
  New widows howl, new orphans cry, new sorrows
  Strike heaven on the face, that it resounds
  As if it felt with Scotland and yell'd out
  Like syllable of dolour.

Malcolm.   What I believe, I'll wail;
  What know, believe; and what I can redress,
  As I shall find the time to friend, I will.
  What you have spoke, it may be so, perchance.
  This tyrant, whose sole name blisters our tongues,
  Was once thought honest: you have loved him well;
  He hath not touch'd you yet. I am young; but something
  You may deserve of him through me; and wisdom
  To offer up a weak, poor, innocent lamb
  To appease an angry god.

Macduff. I am not treacherous.

Malcolm.   But Macbeth is.
  A good and virtuous nature may recoil
  In an imperial charge. But I shall crave your pardon;
  That which you are, my thoughts cannot transpose:
  Angels are bright still, though the brightest fell:
  Though all things foul would wear the brows of grace,
  Yet grace must still look so.

Macduff.   I have lost my hopes.

Malcolm. Perchance even there where I did find my doubts.
  Why in that rawness left you wife and child,
  Those precious motives, those strong knots of love,
  Without leave-taking? I pray you,
  Let not my jealousies be your dishonours,
  But mine own safeties. You may be rightly just,
  Whatever I shall think.

Macduff.   Bleed, bleed, poor country:
  Great tyranny, lay thou thy basis sure,
  For goodness dare not check thee: wear thou thy wrongs;
  The title is affeer'd. Fare thee well, lord:
  I would not be the villain that thou think'st
  For the whole space that's in the tyrant's grasp
  And the rich East to boot.

Malcolm.   Be not offended:
  I speak not as in absolute fear of you.
  I think our country sinks beneath the yoke;
  It weeps, it bleeds, and each new day a gash
  Is added to her wounds: I think withal
  There would be hands uplifted in my right;
  And here from gracious England have I offer
  Of goodly thousands: but for all this,
  When I shall tread upon the tyrant's head,
  Or wear it on my sword, yet my poor country
  Shall have more vices than it had before,
  More suffer and more sundry ways than ever,
  By him that shall succeed.

Macduff.   What should he be?

Malcolm. It is myself I mean: in whom I know
  All the particulars of vice so grafted
  That, when they shall be open'd, black Macbeth

Will seem as pure as snow, and the poor state
Esteem him as a lamb, being compared
With my confineless harms.

Macduff.   Not in the legions
Of horrid hell can come a devil more damn'd
In evils to top Macbeth.

Malcolm.   I grant him bloody,
Luxurious, avaricious, false, deceitful,
Sudden, malicious, smacking of every sin
That has a name: but there's no bottom, none,
In my vulptuousness: your wives, your daughters,
Your matrons and your maids, could not fill up
The cistern of my lust, and my desire
All continent impediments would o'erbear,
That did oppose my will: better Macbeth
Than such an one to reign.

Macduff.   Boundless intemperance
In nature is a tyranny; it hath been
The untimely emptying of the happy throne,
And fall of many kings. But fear not yet
To take upon you what is yours: you may
Convey your pleasures in a spacious plenty,
And yet seem cold, the time you may so hoodwink:
We have willing dames enough; there cannot be
That vulture in you, to devour so many
As will to greatness dedicate themselves,
Finding it so inclined.

Malcolm.   With this there grows
In my most ill-composed affection such
A stanchless avarice that, were I king,
I should cut off the nobles for their lands,
Desire his jewels and this other's house:

And my more-having would be as a sauce
To make me hunger more, that I should forge
Quarrels unjust against the good and loyal,
Destroying them for wealth.

Macduff.   This avarice
Sticks deeper, grows with more pernicious root
Than summer-seeming lust, and it hath been
The sword of our slain kings: yet do not fear;
Scotland hath foisons to fill up your will
Of your mere own: all these are portable,
With other graces weigh'd.

Malcolm. But I have none: the king-becoming graces,
As justice, verity, temperance, stableness,
Bounty, perseverance, mercy, lowliness,
Devotion, patience, courage, fortitude,
I have no relish of them, but abound
In the division of each several crime,
Acting it many ways. Nay, had I power, I should
Pour the sweet milk of concord into hell,
Uproar the universal peace, confound
All unity on earth.

Macduff.   O Scotland, Scotland!

Malcolm. If such a one be fit to govern, speak:
I am as I have spoken.

Macduff.   Fit to govern?
No, not to live. O nation miserable!
With an untitled tyrant bloody-scepter'd,
When shalt thou see thy wholesome days again,
Since that the truest issue of thy throne
By his own interdiction stands accursed,
And does blaspheme his breed? Thy royal father
Was a most sainted king: the queen that bore thee,

Oftener upon her knees than on her feet,
Died every day she lived. Fare thee well!
These evils thou repeat'st upon thyself
Have banish'd me from Scotland. O my breast,
Thy hope ends here!

Malcolm.   Macduff, this noble passion,
Child of integrity, hath from my soul
Wiped the black scruples, reconciled my thoughts
To thy good truth and honour. Devilish Macbeth
By many of these trains hath sought to win me
Into his power; and modest wisdom plucks me
From over-credulous haste: but God above
Deal between thee and me! for even now
I put myself to thy direction, and
Unspeak mine own detraction; here abjure
The taints and blames I laid upon myself,
For strangers to my nature. I am yet
Unknown to woman, never was forsworn,
Scarcely have coveted what was mine own,
At no time broke my faith, would not betray
The Devil to his fellow, and delight
No less in truth than life: my first false speaking
Was this upon myself: what I am truly,
Is thine and my poor country's to command:
Whither indeed, before thy here-approach,
Old Siward, with ten thousand warlike men,
Already at a point, was setting forth.
Now we'll together, and the chance of goodness
Be like our warranted quarrel! Why are you silent?

Macduff. Such welcome and unwelcome things at once
'Tis hard to reconcile.

Enter a Doctor

Malcolm. Well, more anon. Comes the king forth, I pray you?

Doctor. Ay, sir; there are a crew of wretched souls
    That stay his cure: their malady convinces
    The great assay of art; but at his touch,
    Such sanctity hath heaven given his hand,
    They presently amend.

Malcolm.   I thank you, doctor.

                       Exit Doctor.

Macduff. What's the disease he means?

Malcolm.   'Tis call'd the evil:
    A most miraculous work in this good king;
    Which often, since my here-remain in England,
    I have seen him do. How he solicits heaven,
    Himself best knows: but strangely-visited people,
    All swoln and ulcerous, pitiful to the eye,
    The mere despair of surgery, he cures,
    Hanging a golden stamp about their necks,
    Put on with holy prayers: and 'tis spoken,
    To the succeeding royalty he leaves
    The healing benediction. With this strange virtue
    He hath a heavenly gift of prophecy,
    And sundry blessings hang about his throne
    That speak him full of grace.

Enter Ross

Macduff.   See, who comes here?

Malcolm. My countryman; but yet I know him not.

Macduff. My ever gentle cousin, welcome hither.

Malcolm. I know him now: good God, betimes remove
    The means that makes us strangers!

Ross.   Sir, amen.

Macduff. Stands Scotland where it did?

Ross.   Alas, poor country!
  Almost afraid to know itself! It cannot
  Be call'd our mother, but our grave: where nothing,
  But who knows nothing, is once seen to smile;
  Where sighs and groans, and shrieks that rend the air,
  Are made, not mark'd; where violent sorrow seems
  A modern ecstasy: the dead man's knell
  Is there scarce ask'd for who; and good men's lives
  Expire before the flowers in their caps,
  Dying or ere they sicken.

Macduff.   O, relation
  Too nice, and yet too true!

Malcolm.   What's the newest grief?

Ross. That of an hour's age doth hiss the speaker;
  Each minute teems a new one.

Macduff.   How does my wife?

Ross. Why, well.

Macduff.   And all my children?

Ross.   Well too.

Macduff. The tyrant has not batter'd at their peace?

Ross. No; they were well at peace when I did leave 'em.

Macduff. Be not a niggard of your speech: how goes 't?

Ross. When I came hither to transport the tidings,
  Which I have heavily borne, there ran a rumour
  Of many worthy fellows that were out;
  Which was to my belief witness'd the rather,
  For that I saw the tyrant's power a-foot:
  Now is the time of help; your eye in Scotland

Would create soldiers, make our women fight,
To doff their dire distresses.

Malcolm.   Be 't their comfort
We are coming thither: gracious England hath
Lent us good Siward and ten thousand men;
An older and a better soldier none
That Christendom gives out.

Ross.   Would I could answer
This comfort with the like! But I have words
That would be howl'd out in the desert air,
Where hearing should not latch them.

Macduff.   What concern they?
The general cause? or is it a fee-grief
Due to some single breast?

Ross.   No mind that's honest
But in it shares some woe, though the main part
Pertains to you alone.

Macduff.   If it be mine,
Keep it not from me, quickly let me have it.

Ross. Let not your ears despise my tongue for ever,
Which shall possess them with the heaviest sound
That ever yet they heard.

Macduff.   Hum! I guess at it.

Ross. Your castle is surprised; your wife and babes
Savagely slaughter'd: to relate the manner,
Were, on the quarry of these murder'd deer,
To add the death of you.

Malcolm.   Merciful heaven!
What, man! ne'er pull your hat upon your brows;
Give sorrow words: the grief that does not speak
Whispers the o'er-fraught heart, and bids it break.

Macduff. My children too?

Ross.   Wife, children, servants, all
That could be found.

Macduff.   And I must be from thence!
My wife kill'd too?

Ross.   I have said.

Malcolm.   Be comforted:
Let's make us medicines of our great revenge,
To cure this deadly grief.

Macduff. He has no children. All my pretty ones?
Did you say all? O hell-kite! All?
What, all my pretty chickens and their dam
At one fell swoop?

Malcolm. Dispute it like a man.

Macduff.   I shall do so;
But I must also feel it as a man:
I cannot but remember such things were,
That were most precious to me. Did heaven look on,
And would not take their part? Sinful Macduff,
They were all struck for thee! naught that I am,
Not for their own demerits, but for mine,
Fell slaughter on their souls: heaven rest them now!

Malcolm. Be this the whetstone of your sword: let grief
Convert to anger; blunt not the heart, enrage it.

Macduff. O, I could play the woman with mine eyes,
And braggart with my tongue! But, gentle heavens,
Cut short all intermission; front to front
Bring thou this fiend of Scotland and myself;
Within my sword's length set him; if he 'scape,
Heaven forgive him too!

Malcolm.   This tune goes manly.
  Come, go we to the king; our power is ready;
  Our lack is nothing but our leave. Macbeth
  Is ripe for shaking, and the Powers above
  Put on their instruments. Receive what cheer you may;
  The night is long that never finds the day.

                                        Exeunt.

act 5

scene 1. [*Dunsinane. Ante-room in the castle*]

Enter a Doctor of Physic *and a* Waiting-Gentlewoman

Doctor. I have two nights watched with you, but can perceive no truth in your report. When was it she last walked?

Gentlewoman. Since his majesty went into the field, I have seen her rise from her bed, throw her nightgown upon her, unlock her closet, take forth paper, fold it, write upon 't, read it, afterwards seal it, and again return to bed; yet all this while in a most fast sleep.

Doctor. A great perturbation in nature, to receive at once the benefit of sleep and do the effects of watching. In this slumbery agitation, besides her walking and other actual performances, what, at any time, have you heard her say?

Gentlewoman. That, sir, which I will not report after her.

Doctor. You may to me, and 'tis most meet you should.

Gentlewoman. Neither to you nor any one, having no witness to confirm my speech.

Enter Lady Macbeth, *with a taper*

Lo you, here she comes! This is her very guise, and,
upon my life, fast asleep. Observe her; stand close.

Doctor. How came she by that light?

Gentlewoman. Why, it stood by her: she has light by her
continually; 'tis her command.

Doctor. You see, her eyes are open.

Gentlewoman. Ay, but their sense is shut.

Doctor. What is it she does now? Look, how she rubs her hands.

Gentlewoman. It is an accustomed action with her, to seem thus
washing her hands: I have known her continue in this a
quarter of an hour.

Lady Macbeth. Yet here's a spot.

Doctor. Hark! she speaks: I will set down what comes from her,
to satisfy my remembrance the more strongly.

Lady Macbeth. Out, damned spot! out, I say! One: two: why, then
'tis time to do 't. Hell is murky. Fie, my lord, fie! a soldier,
and afeard? What need we fear who knows it, when none can
call our power to accompt? Yet who would have thought the
old man to have had so much blood in him?

Doctor. Do you mark that?

Lady Macbeth. The thane of Fife had a wife; where is she now?
What, will these hands ne'er be clean? No more o' that,
my lord, no more o' that: you mar all with this starting.

Doctor. Go to, go to; you have known what you should not.

Gentlewoman. She has spoke what she should not, I am sure of
that: heaven knows what she has known.

Lady Macbeth. Here's the smell of the blood still: all the perfumes
of Arabia will not sweeten this little hand. Oh, oh, oh!

Doctor. What a sigh is there! The heart is sorely charged.

Gentlewoman. I would not have such a heart in my bosom for the dignity of the whole body.

Doctor. Well, well, well,—

Gentlewoman. Pray God it be, sir.

Doctor. This disease is beyond my practice: yet I have known those which have walked in their sleep who have died holily in their beds.

Lady Macbeth. Wash your hands; put on your nightgown; look not so pale: I tell you yet again, Banquo's buried; he cannot come out on 's grave.

Doctor. Even so?

Lady Macbeth. To bed, to bed; there's knocking at the gate: come, come, come, come, give me your hand: what's done cannot be undone: to bed, to bed, to bed.

Exit.

Doctor. Will she go now to bed?

Gentlewoman. Directly.

Doctor. Foul whisp'rings are abroad: unnatural deeds
Do breed unnatural troubles: infected minds
To their deaf pillows will discharge their secrets:
More needs she the divine than the physician.
God, God forgive us all! Look after her;
Remove from her the means of all annoyance,
And still keep eyes upon her. So good night:
My mind she has mated, and amazed my sight:
I think, but dare not speak.

Gentlewoman.   Good night, good doctor.

Exeunt.

scene 2. [*The country near Dunsinane*]

Drum and colours. Enter Menteith, Caithness, Angus,
Lennox, *and* Soldiers

Menteith. The English power is near, led on by Malcolm,
His uncle Siward and the good Macduff:
Revenges burn in them; for their dear causes
Would to the bleeding and the grim alarm
Excite the mortified man.

Angus.   Near Birnam wood
Shall we well meet them; that way are they coming.

Caithness. Who knows if Donalbain be with his brother?

Lennox. For certain, sir, he is not: I have a file
Of all the gentry: there is Siward's son,
And many unrough youths, that even now
Protest their first of manhood.

Menteith.   What does the tyrant?

Caithness. Great Dunsinane he strongly fortifies:
Some say he's mad; others, that lesser hate him,
Do call it valiant fury: but, for certain,
He cannot buckle his distemper'd cause
Within the belt of rule.

Angus.   Now does he feel
His secret murders sticking on his hands;
Now minutely revolts upbraid his faith-breach;
Those he commands move only in command,
Nothing in love: now does he feel his title
Hang loose about him, like a giant's robe
Upon a dwarfish thief.

Menteith.   Who then shall blame
    His pester'd senses to recoil and start,
    When all that is within him does condemn
    Itself for being there?

Caithness.   Well, march we on,
    To give obedience where 'tis truly owed:
    Meet we the medicine of the sickly weal,
    And with him pour we, in our country's purge,
    Each drop of us.

Lennox.   Or so much as it needs
    To dew the sovereign flower and drown the weeds.
    Make we our march towards Birnam.

                                Exeunt, marching.

scene 3.   [*Dunsinane. A room in the castle*]

Enter Macbeth, Doctor, *and* Attendants

Macbeth. Bring me no more reports; let them fly all:
    Till Birnam wood remove to Dunsinane
    I cannot taint with fear. What's the boy Malcolm?
    Was he not born of woman? The spirits that know
    All mortal consequences have pronounced me thus:
    'Fear not, Macbeth; no man that's born of woman
    Shall e'er have power upon thee.' Then fly, false thanes,
    And mingle with the English epicures:
    The mind I sway by and the heart I bear
    Shall never sag with doubt nor shake with fear.
                     Enter a Servant
    The devil damn thee black; thou cream-faced loon!
    Where got'st thou that goose look?

Servant. There is ten thousand—

Macbeth.   Geese, villain?

Servant.   Soldiers, sir.

Macbeth. Go prick thy face and over-red thy fear,
Thou lily-liver'd boy. What soldiers, patch?
Death of thy soul! those linen cheeks of thine
Are counsellors to fear. What soldiers, whey-face?

Servant. The English force, so please you.

Macbeth. Take thy face hence.

Exit Servant.
                    Seyton!—I am sick at heart,
When I behold—Seyton, I say!—This push
Will cheer me ever, or disseat me now.
I have lived long enough: my way of life
Is fall'n into the sere, the yellow leaf,
And that which should accompany old age,
As honour, love, obedience, troops of friends,
I must not look to have; but, in their stead,
Curses, not loud but deep, mouth-honour, breath,
Which the poor heart would fain deny, and dare not.
Seyton!

Enter Seyton

Seyton.   What's your gracious pleasure?

Macbeth.   What news more?

Seyton. All is confirm'd, my lord, which was reported.

Macbeth. I'll fight, till from my bones my flesh be hack'd.
Give me my armour.

Seyton.   'Tis not needed yet.

Macbeth. I'll put it on.
Send out moe horses, skirr the country round;
Hang those that talk of fear. Give me mine armour.
How does your patient, doctor?

Doctor. Not so sick, my lord,
As she is troubled with thick–coming fancies,
That keep her from her rest.

Macbeth. Cure her of that.
Canst thou not minister to a mind diseased,
Pluck from the memory a rooted sorrow,
Raze out the written troubles of the brain,
And with some sweet oblivious antidote
Cleanse the stuff'd bosom of that perilous stuff
Which weighs upon the heart?

Doctor. Therein the patient
Must minister to himself.

Macbeth. Throw physic to the dogs, I'll none of it.
Come, put mine armour on; give me my staff.
Seyton, send out. Doctor, the thanes fly from me.
Come, sir, dispatch. If thou couldst, doctor, cast
The water of my land, find her disease
And purge it to a sound and pristine health,
I would applaud thee to the very echo,
That should applaud again. Pull 't off, I say.
What rhubarb, senna, or what purgative drug,
Would scour these English hence? Hear'st thou of them?

Doctor. Ay, my good lord; your royal preparation
Makes us hear something.

Macbeth. Bring it after me.
I will not be afraid of death and bane
Till Birnam forest come to Dunsinane.

Doctor. [*Aside*] Were I from Dunsinane away and clear,
Profit again should hardly draw me here.

Exeunt.

scene 4. [*Country near Birnam wood*]

Drum and colours. Enter Malcolm, *old* Siward *and his*
Son, Macduff, Menteith, Caithness, Angus, Lennox,
Ross, *and* Soldiers, *marching*

Malcolm. Cousins, I hope the days are near at hand,
That chambers will be safe.

Menteith.   We doubt it nothing.

Siward. What wood is this before us?

Menteith.   The wood of Birnam.

Malcolm. Let every soldier hew him down a bough,
And bear 't before him: thereby shall we shadow
The numbers of our host, and make discovery
Err in report of us.

Soldiers.   It shall be done.

Siward. We learn no other but the confident tyrant
Keeps still in Dunsinane, and will endure
Our setting down before 't.

Malcolm.   'Tis his main hope:
For where there is advantage to be given,
Both more and less have given him the revolt,
And none serve with him but constrained things
Whose hearts are absent too.

Macduff.   Let our just censures
Attend the true event, and put we on
Industrious soldiership.

Siward.   The time approaches,
That will with due decision make us know

What we shall say we have and what we owe.
Thoughts speculative their unsure hopes relate,
But certain issue strokes must arbitrate:
Towards which advance the war.

Exeunt, marching.

scene 5.   [*Dunsinane. Within the castle*]

Enter Macbeth, Seyton, *and* Soldiers, *with drum and colours*

Macbeth. Hang out our banners on the outward walls;
    The cry is still 'They come:' our castle's strength
    Will laugh a siege to scorn: here let them lie
    Till famine and the ague eat them up:
    Were they not forced with those that should be ours,
    We might have met them dareful, beard to beard,
    And beat them backward home.

A cry of women within.
                                What is that noise?

Seyton. It is the cry of women, my good lord.

Exit.

Macbeth. I have almost forgot the taste of fears:
    The time has been, my senses would have cool'd
    To hear a night-shriek, and my fell of hair
    Would at a dismal treatise rouse and stir
    As life were in 't: I have supp'd full with horrors;
    Direness, familiar to my slaughterous thoughts,
    Cannot once start me.

Re-enter Seyton
                Wherefore was that cry?

Seyton. The queen, my lord, is dead.

Macbeth. She should have died hereafter;

There would have been a time for such a word.
To-morrow, and to-morrow, and to-morrow,
Creeps in this petty pace from day to day,
To the last syllable of recorded time;
And all our yesterdays have lighted fools
The way to dusty death. Out, out, brief candle!
Life's but a walking shadow, a poor player
That struts and frets his hour upon the stage
And then is heard no more: it is a tale
Told by an idiot, full of sound and fury,
Signifying nothing.

Enter a Messenger

Thou comest to use thy tongue; thy story quickly.

Messenger. Gracious my lord,
I should report that which I say I saw,
But know not how to do it.

Macbeth.   Well, say, sir.

Messenger. As I did stand my watch upon the hill,
I look'd toward Birnam, and anon, methought,
The wood began to move.

Macbeth.   Liar and slave!

Messenger. Let me endure your wrath, if 't be not so:
Within this three mile may you see it coming;
I say, a moving grove.

Macbeth.   If thou speak'st false,
Upon the next tree shalt thou hang alive,
Till famine cling thee: if thy speech be sooth,
I care not if thou dost for me as much.
I pull in resolution, and begin
To doubt the equivocation of the fiend
That lies like truth: 'Fear not, till Birnam wood

Do come to Dunsinane;' and now a wood
Comes toward Dunsinane. Arm, arm, and out!
If this which he avouches does appear,
There is nor flying hence nor tarrying here.
I 'gin to be a-weary of the sun,
And wish the estate o' the world were now undone.
Ring the alarum-bell! Blow, wind! come, wrack!
At least we'll die with harness on our back.

Exeunt.

scene 6. [*Dunsinane. Before the castle*]

Drum and colours. Enter Malcolm, *old* Siward, Macduff, *and their*
Army, *with boughs*

Malcolm. Now near enough; your leavy screens throw down,
And show like those you are. You, worthy uncle,
Shall, with my cousin, your right noble son,
Lead our first battle: worthy Macduff and we
Shall take upon 's what else remains to do,
According to our order.

Siward.   Fare you well.
Do we but find the tyrant's power to-night,
Let us be beaten, if we cannot fight.

Macduff. Make all our trumpets speak; give them all breath,
Those clamorous harbingers of blood and death.

Exeunt.

scene 7. [*Another part of the field*]

Alarums. Enter Macbeth

Macbeth. They have tied me to a stake; I cannot fly,
  But bear-like I must fight the course. What's he
  That was not born of woman? Such a one
  Am I to fear, or none.

Enter Young Siward

Young Siward. What is thy name?

Macbeth.   Thou'lt be afraid to hear it.

Young Siward. No; though thou call'st thyself a hotter name
  Than any is in hell.

Macbeth.   My name's Macbeth.

Young Siward. The devil himself could not pronounce a title
  More hateful to mine ear.

Macbeth.   No, nor more fearful.

Young Siward. Thou liest, abhorred tyrant; with my sword
  I'll prove the lie thou speak'st.

They fight, and Young Siward *is slain.*

Macbeth.   Thou wast born of woman.
  But swords I smile at, weapons laugh to scorn,
  Brandish'd by man that's of a woman born.

Exit.

Alarums. Enter Macduff

Macduff. That way the noise is. Tyrant, show thy face!
  If thou be'st slain and with no stroke of mine,
  My wife and children's ghosts will haunt me still.
  I cannot strike at wretched kerns, whose arms

Are hired to bear their staves: either thou, Macbeth,
Or else my sword, with an unbatter'd edge,
I sheathe again undeeded. There thou shouldst be;
By this great clatter, one of greatest note
Seems bruited: let me find him, Fortune!
And more I beg not.

Exit. Alarums.

Enter Malcolm *and old* Siward

Siward. This way, my lord; the castle's gently render'd:
The tyrant's people on both sides do fight;
The noble thanes do bravely in the war;
The day almost itself professes yours,
And little is to do.

Malcolm. We have met with foes
That strike beside us.

Siward. Enter, sir, the castle.

Exeunt. Alarum.

scene 8. [*Another part of the field*]

Enter Macbeth

Macbeth. Why should I play the Roman fool, and die
On mine own sword? whiles I see lives, the gashes
Do better upon them.

Enter Macduff

Macduff. Turn, Hell–hound, turn!

Macbeth. Of all men else I have avoided thee:
But get thee back; my soul is too much charged
With blood of thine already.

Macduff. I have no words:

My voice is in my sword, thou bloodier villain
Than terms can give thee out!

They fight.

Macbeth.   Thou losest labour:
As easy mayst thou the intrenchant air
With thy keen sword impress as make me bleed:
Let fall thy blade on vulnerable crests;
I bear a charmed life, which must not yield
To one of woman born.

Macduff.   Despair thy charm,
And let the angel whom thou still hast served
Tell thee, Macduff was from his mother's womb
Untimely ripp'd.

Macbeth. Accursed be that tongue that tells me so,
For it hath cow'd my better part of man!
And be these juggling fiends no more believed,
That palter with us in a double sense;
That keep the word of promise to our ear,
And break it to our hope. I'll not fight with thee.

Macduff. Then yield thee, coward,
And live to be the show and gaze o' the time:
We'll have thee, as our rarer monsters are,
Painted upon a pole, and underwrit,
'Here may you see the tyrant.'

Macbeth.   I will not yield,
To kiss the ground before young Malcolm's feet,
And to be baited with the rabble's curse.
Though Birnam wood be come to Dunsinane,
And thou opposed, being of no woman born,
Yet I will try the last: before my body
I throw my warlike shield: lay on, Macduff;

And damn'd be him that first cries 'Hold, enough!'

Exeunt, fighting. Alarums.

Retreat, Flourish. Enter, with drum and colours,
Malcolm, *old* Siward, Ross, *the other* Thanes,
and Soldiers

Malcolm. I would the friends we miss were safe arrived.

Siward. Some must go off: and yet, by these I see,
So great a day as this is cheaply bought.

Malcolm. Macduff is missing, and your noble son.

Ross. Your son, my lord, has paid a soldier's debt:
He only lived but till he was a man;
The which no sooner had his prowess confirm'd
In the unshrinking station where he fought,
But like a man he died.

Siward. Then he is dead?

Ross. Ay, and brought off the field: your cause of sorrow
Must not be measured by his worth, for then
It hath no end.

Siward. Had he his hurts before?

Ross. Ay, on the front.

Siward. Why then, God's soldier be he!
Had I as many sons as I have hairs,
I would not wish them to a fairer death:
And so his knell is knoll'd.

Malcolm. He's worth more sorrow,
And that I'll spend for him.

Siward. He's worth no more:
They say he parted well and paid his score:
And so God be with him! Here comes newer comfort.

Re-enter Macduff, *with* Macbeth's *head*

Macduff. Hail, king! for so thou art: behold, where stands
　　Th'usurper's cursed head : the time is free.
　　I see thee compass'd with thy kingdom's pearl,
　　That speak my salutation in their minds;
　　Whose voices I desire aloud with mine,—
　　Hail, King of Scotland!

All.　　　　　　　　　Hail, King of Scotland!

　　　　　　　　　　　　　　　　Flourish.

Malcolm. We shall not spend a large expense of time
　　Before we reckon with your several loves,
　　And make us even with you. My thanes and kinsmen,
　　Henceforth be earls, the first that ever Scotland
　　In such an honour named. What's more to do,
　　Which would be planted newly with the time,
　　As calling home our exiled friends abroad
　　That fled the snares of watchful tyranny,
　　Producing forth the cruel ministers
　　Of this dead butcher and his fiend-like queen,
　　Who, as 'tis thought, by self and violent hands
　　Took off her life; this, and what needful else
　　That calls upon us, by the grace of Grace
　　We will perform in measure, time, and place:
　　So thanks to all at once and to each one,
　　Whom we invite to see us crown'd at Scone.

　　　　　　　　　　　　　Flourish. Exeunt.